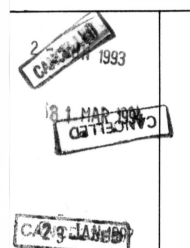

CAMBRIDGE TEXTBOOKS IN LINGUISTICS

General Editors: W. SYDNEY ALLEN, B. COMRIE
C. J. FILLMORE, E. J. A. HENDERSON, F. W. HOUSEHOLDER
R. LASS, J. LYONS, R. B. LE PAGE, P. H. MATTHEWS, R. POSNER,
J. L. M. TRIM

ASPECT

In this series

P. H. MATTHEWS *Morphology*
B. COMRIE *Aspect*
R. M. KEMPSON *Semantic Theory*
T. BYNON *Historical Linguistics*
J. ALLWOOD, L.-G. ANDERSSON, Ö. DAHL *Logic in Linguistics*
D. B. FRY *The Physics of Speech*
R. A. HUDSON *Sociolinguistics*

ASPECT

AN INTRODUCTION TO
THE STUDY OF VERBAL ASPECT
AND RELATED PROBLEMS

BERNARD COMRIE

LECTURER IN LINGUISTICS
UNIVERSITY OF CAMBRIDGE

CAMBRIDGE UNIVERSITY PRESS
CAMBRIDGE
LONDON   NEW YORK   NEW ROCHELLE
MELBOURNE   SYDNEY

Published by the Press Syndicate of the University of Cambridge
The Pitt Building, Trumpington Street, Cambridge CB2 1RP
32 East 57th Street, New York, NY 10022, USA
296 Beaconsfield Parade, Middle Park, Melbourne 3206, Australia

© Cambridge University Press 1976

Library of Congress catalogue card number: 75-44577

First published 1976
Reprinted with corrections 1978, 1981

Printed in Great Britain at the
University Press, Cambridge

Library of Congress Cataloguing in Publication Data

Comrie, Bernard, 1947–

Aspect.

(Cambridge textbooks in linguistics)

Bibliography: p.

Includes index.

1. Grammar, Comparative and general – Aspect.

I. Title.

P281.C6   415   75-44577

ISBN 0 521 21109 3   hard covers
ISBN 0 521 29045 7   paperback

CONTENTS

Preface vii   *Abbreviations* ix

Introduction   *page* 1
0.1 *Definition of aspect*   1
0.2 *Meaning and form*   6
0.3 *Terminology*   11
0.4 *Structure of the book*   13
0.5 *General reading*   14

1   Perfective and imperfective   16
1.1 *Perfective*   16
1.1.1 *Definition of perfectivity*   16
1.1.2 *Perfectivity and other aspectual values* 21
1.2 *Imperfective*   24
1.2.1 *Habitual*   26
.2.1.1 *Habitual and other aspectual values*   30
1.2.2 *Progressive*   32

2   Aspect and inherent meaning   41
2.1 *Punctual and durative*   41
2.2 *Telic and atelic*   44
2.3 *State and dynamic situation*   48

3   Perfect   52
3.1 *Types of perfect*   56
3.1.1 *Perfect of result*   56
3.1.2 *Experiential perfect*   58
3.1.3 *Perfect of persistent situation*   60
3.1.4 *Perfect of recent past*   60
3.2 *Perfect and other aspects*   61
3.3 *Prospective aspect*   64

4   Aspect and tense   66
4.1 *Perfective, present, and future*   66
4.2 *Aspectual distinctions restricted to certain tenses* 71

4.3	*Narrative Present*	*page* 73
4.4	*Combined tense/aspect oppositions*	78
4.5	*Aspect and time reference in tenseless languages*	82
4.6	*Aspect and voice*	84
5	Formal expression of aspectual oppositions	87
5.1	*Morphology of aspect*	87
5.1.1	*Prefixing in Balto-Slavonic, Georgian, and Hungarian*	88
5.1.2	*Combined tense/aspect morphology*	94
5.2	*Syntactic expressions of aspectual oppositions*	98
5.2.1	*Locative expressions of aspectual oppositions*	98
5.2.1.1	*Progressive and imperfective aspect*	98
5.2.1.2	*Contingent state*	103
5.2.1.3	*Direction and aspect*	106
5.2.2	*Perfect as present plus past*	106
5.2.2.1	*Perfect and inferential*	108
6	Markedness	111
6.1	*Markedness and semantics*	112
6.2	*Markedness and morphology*	114
6.3	*Neutralisation*	116
6.4	*Markedness and frequency*	116
6.5	*Markedness and context*	118
6.6	*Degree of markedness*	122
	Appendix A Language guide	123
A.1	*Genetic classification of languages cited*	123
A.2	*Aspectual systems of individual languages*	124
A.2.1	*English*	124
A.2.2	*Slavonic (Russian, Bulgarian, Old Church Slavonic)*	125
A.2.3	*Romance (French, Spanish)*	126
A.2.4	*Greek (Ancient Greek, Modern Greek)*	127
A.2.5	*Chinese (Mandarin)*	128
A.2.6	*Other languages (Turkish, ChiBemba)*	128
	Appendix B Recent approaches to aspect	129
B.1	*Localist theory of aspect*	129
B.2	*Feature analysis*	130
B.3	*Model-theoretic semantics*	132
	References	134
	Index	139

PREFACE

The aim of the present book is to provide an introduction to verbal aspect and related concepts. It differs from most other books on aspect in that it is not concerned with any one particular language, nor with a comparison of various individual languages, but rather presents aspect as a part of general linguistic theory. Theoretical points are, of course, illustrated throughout with examples from various languages: English, as the language that all readers of the book will have in common; Russian and other Slavonic languages, in view of the importance of data from these languages in the development of the study of aspect, and also as these are the foreign languages most familiar to the author; the Romance languages (in particular, French and Spanish); as well as a variety of other languages, ranging from Greek to Chinese. References are made throughout to descriptive works dealing with the various languages alluded to.

The book does not presuppose any previous knowledge of aspect, although it does assume that the reader has the sort of background that can be expected of someone who has followed an introductory course in general linguistics, or is following such a course, and is prepared to consult other textbooks and reference works for further details of general theoretical points. It does not attempt to put across any one particular current approach to the problem of aspect, although it does aim at internal consistency, nor does it provide a historical résumé of the various approaches that have been proposed. Most of the discussion is cast in the general terms of traditional grammar, paying particular attention to the semantics of aspect. In addition, attention is paid to some of the achievements of the structuralist approach to aspect (especially chapter 6 on markedness), and of the philosophical approach (especially chapter 2 on aspect and inherent meaning). An appendix (appendix B) outlines three recent approaches to the analysis of aspect, to give the reader some idea of current work in this field.

I shall consider the purpose of this book to be fulfilled if it gives its readers a greater awareness of the problem of aspect, and conveys to them the general concepts concerned, even more so if they then go on to apply this knowledge in their work on the languages that particularly interest them.

I am grateful to the following, who either provided me with bibliographic references, volunteered information about the aspectual systems of various languages, answered my more specific questions, or discussed general and specific problems of aspect with me: G. M. Awbery, W. S. Allen, E. W. Browne, M. Harris, M. Ivić, and J. Miller. I am particularly grateful to J. Lyons, who read an earlier draft of this book and made detailed comments on it. The responsibility for accepting or rejecting their suggestions is, of course, my own.

Part of the preparation of this book was carried out while I was a Research Fellow at King's College, Cambridge.

June 1975   Bernard Comrie

PREFACE TO THE SECOND PRINTING

In addition to removing a few misprints, I have corrected an error in the discussion of Bulgarian (p. 109) and a non-sequitur in the discussion of Irish and Scots Gaelic (p. 104), both brought to my attention by E. W. Browne, and have amended the Hungarian examples on p. 93 at the suggestion of P. Sherwood.

January 1978   Bernard Comrie

PREFACE TO THE THIRD PRINTING

Amendments have been limited to the correction of minor errors in the Portuguese examples on pp. 23, 34, 35 and 105, the Irish example on p. 39 (brought to my attention by G. Geoghgan-Dubois), the Arabic examples on pp. 79–81, and the discussion of Georgian on p. 100 (at the suggestion of D. A. Holisky).

June 1980   Bernard Comrie

ABBREVIATIONS

In example sentences and glosses, the abbreviations Ipfv., for Imperfective, and Pfv., for Perfective, are used throughout.

An asterisk before a sentence or other form indicates ungrammaticality; a question-mark indicates dubious grammaticality.

Introduction

0.1. Definition of aspect

Since the term 'aspect' tends to be less familiar to students of linguistics than are terms for the other verbal categories such as tense or mood, it is as well, before giving a definition of aspect, to consider some examples of aspectual distinctions in languages likely to be familiar to readers, in order to provide some factual material against which it will be possible to view the more theoretical part of the discussion.

Students of Russian and other Slavonic languages are familiar with the distinction between Perfective and Imperfective aspect, as in *on pročital* (Pfv.) and *on čital* (Ipfv.), both translatable into English as 'he read', although some idea of the difference can be given by translating the Imperfective as 'he was reading, he used to read'; this is only an approximate characterisation, and a more detailed discussion will be found in the body of the book. In fact, the distinction between *he read, he was reading*, and *he used to read* in English is equally an aspectual distinction, so aspect is a category even in as familiar a language as English. Similarly in the Romance languages, the difference between, for instance, French *il lut* and *il lisait*, Spanish *leyó* and *(él) leía*, Italian *lesse* and *leggeva*, is one of aspect, despite the traditional terminology, which speaks of the Imperfect (*lisait, leía, leggeva*) as a tense, and equally of the Simple Past (*lut, leyó, lesse*), also called the Past Definite, Historic, or Remote, as a tense.[1]

Particularly in view of this terminological, and conceptual, confusion of tense and aspect, it is worth ensuring now that the meaning of the more familiar term 'tense' is understood, before embarking on discussion of the less familiar term 'aspect'. Tense relates the time of the

---

[1] An explanation for the traditional confusion between aspect and tense in speaking of the Romance past tense forms is suggested in section 5.1.2.

situation referred to to some other time, usually to the moment of speaking.[1] The commonest tenses found in languages – though not all languages distinguish these three tenses, or indeed distinguish tense at all – are present, past, and future: a situation described in the present tense is located temporally as simultaneous with the moment of speaking (e.g. *John is singing*); one described in the past as located prior to the moment of speaking (e.g. *John sang, John was singing*); one described in the future as located subsequent to the moment of speaking (e.g. *John will sing, John will be singing*).[2] Since tense locates the time of a situation relative to the situation of the utterance, we may describe tense as deictic.[3]

The tenses referred to so far have all related the time of the situation described to the present moment. Such tenses are referred to as absolute tenses. Another possible form of time reference is relative time reference where, instead of the time of a situation being located relative to the present moment, it is related to the time of some other situation. Nonfinite participial constructions in English, for instance, involve relative rather than absolute tense. In the sentences (a) *when walking down the road, I often meet Harry* and (b) *when walking down the road, I often met Harry*, the present participle *walking* in both cases indicates a situation located simultaneous with the time of the main verb, irrespective of the tense of the main verb. In the (a) sentence, the situation described by *walking* holds at the present, given the present tense *meet*, while in the (b) sentence it held in the past, given the past tense *met*; the relevant factor in the choice of the present participle is thus relative time reference, not absolute time reference. Similarly, the so-called perfect participle in such nonfinite participial constructions indicates relative past time reference, e.g. *having met Harry earlier, I don't need to see him again*, versus *having met Harry earlier, I didn't need to see him again*. In English, typically, finite verb forms have absolute tense, and nonfinite verb forms have relative tense. In section 4.4 we shall see that in written Arabic and (Mandarin) Chinese there are verb forms that express relative, rather than absolute, tense; though in the absence of any specification of the time-point relative to which the time reference is made, this time-point is taken to be the present moment.

[1] For further discussion, see, for instance, Lyons (1968: 304–6).

[2] The so-called future tense of many languages has modal as well as tense value; throughout this book the traditional term 'future tense' is used, though it should be borne in mind that this is often as much a mood as a tense. [3] Lyons (1968: 275–81).

Aspect is quite different from this. The difference in French between *il lisait* and *il lut*, or in English between *he was reading* and *he read*, is not one of tense, since in both cases we have absolute past tense. It is in this sense that we speak of aspect as being distinct from tense, and insist on such oppositions as that between perfective and imperfective being treated as aspectual, even where the grammatical terminology of individual languages has a tradition of referring to them as tenses.

As the general definition of aspect, we may take the formulation that 'aspects are different ways of viewing the internal temporal constituency of a situation'.[1] We may illustrate this definition briefly, returning to more detailed exemplification in the body of the book, by considering one of the differences between the aspectual forms given above as examples of aspectual distinctions in various languages, as illustrated in the following translation equivalents:

> English: John was reading when I entered.
> Russian: Ivan čital, kogda ja vošel.
> French: Jean lisait quand j'entrai.
> Spanish: Juan leía cuando entré.
> Italian: Gianni leggeva quando entrai.

In each of these sentences, the first verb presents the background to some event, while that event itself is introduced by the second verb.[2] The second verb presents the totality of the situation referred to (here, my entry) without reference to its internal temporal constituency: the whole of the situation is presented as a single unanalysable whole, with beginning, middle, and end rolled into one; no attempt is made to divide this situation up into the various individual phases that make up the action of entry. Verbal forms with this meaning will be said to have perfective meaning, and where the language in question has special verbal forms to indicate this, we shall say that it has perfective aspect.[3]

---

[1] This is based on the definition given by Holt (1943: 6): 'les manières diverses de concevoir l'écoulement du procès même', i.e. 'different ways of conceiving the flow of the process itself'. This definition has been generalised somewhat so that it does not refer solely to processes, but also, for instance, to states; see further chapter 2.

[2] This is a well established pedagogical technique for introducing the concept of aspect in teaching individual languages with oppositions of this kind. See, for instance, Klein (1974: 98–100).

[3] Of the five languages cited here, all but English have perfective aspect in this sense. In English the relation between the Progressive (e.g. *was reading*) and non-Progressive (e.g. *entered*) is rather more complex, but

3

The other forms, i.e. those referring to the situation of John's reading, do not present the situation in this way, but rather make explicit reference to the internal temporal constituency of the situation. In these examples, in particular, reference is made to an internal portion of John's reading, while there is no explicit reference to the beginning or to the end of his reading. This is why the sentences are interpreted as meaning that my entry is an event that occurred during the period that John was reading, i.e. John's reading both preceded and followed my entry. Another way of explaining the difference between perfective and imperfective meaning is to say that the perfective looks at the situation from outside, without necessarily distinguishing any of the internal structure of the situation, whereas the imperfective looks at the situation from inside, and as such is crucially concerned with the internal structure of the situation, since it can both look backwards towards the start of the situation, and look forwards to the end of the situation, and indeed is equally appropriate if the situation is one that lasts through all time, without any beginning and without any end.

In discussing aspect it is important to grasp that the difference between perfectivity and imperfectivity is not necessarily an objective difference between situations, nor is it necessarily a difference that is presented by the speaker as being objective. It is quite possible for the same speaker to refer to the same situation once with a perfective form, then with an imperfective, without in any way being self-contradictory. This can be illustrated by means of sentences like *John read that book yesterday; while he was reading it, the postman came*, or its equivalents in French (*Jean lut ce livre hier; pendant qu'il le lisait, le facteur vint*) or Russian (*Ivan pročital ètu knigu včera; v to vremja, kogda on ee čital, prišel počtal'on*). The different forms of the verb 'to read' all refer to the same situation of reading. In the first clause, however, John's reading is presented as a complete event, without further subdivision into successive temporal phases; in the second clause, this event is opened up, so that the speaker is now in the middle of the situation of John's reading, and says that it was in the middle of this situation (which he had previously referred to using the form with perfective meaning) that the event of the postman's arrival took place.

provided we restrict ourselves to nonstative verbs and exclude habitual meaning, then the difference between the two forms is one of imperfectivity versus perfectivity, as in the example above. For further discussion, see section 1.2.2 on the progressive.

From the discussion of the previous paragraphs, it will be evident that aspect is not unconnected with time, and the reader may therefore wonder whether this does not vitiate the distinction insisted on above between aspect and tense. However, although both aspect and tense are concerned with time, they are concerned with time in very different ways. As noted above, tense is a deictic category, i.e. locates situations in time, usually with reference to the present moment, though also with reference to other situations. Aspect is not concerned with relating the time of the situation to any other time-point, but rather with the internal temporal constituency of the one situation; one could state the difference as one between situation-internal time (aspect) and situation-external time (tense). In a sentence like *John was reading when I entered* it might seem that the different forms do serve a deictic function of locating my entry internally to John's reading, but this apparent deictic function is only a secondary consequence of the different ways in which they view the internal constituency of the situations referred to: since *was reading* places us internally to the reading situation, therefore naturally when we are presented with another situation given to us as a unified whole without internal constituency, this new situation is located temporally at that point in time where we already are, namely internally to John's reading. Similarly, a sequence of forms with perfective meaning will normally be taken to indicate a sequence of events, e.g. *the wind tore off the roof, snapped the clothes-line, and brought down the apple-tree.* Since each of the three situations is presented without regard to its internal constituency, a natural interpretation is to take them as events that occurred in succession, each one complete in itself; moreover, they will normally be taken to have occurred in the order in which they are presented in the text. However, this is by no means a necessary interpretation. It is quite possible, even if unlikely, for all three events to have been simultaneous, and this possibility can be made explicit by adding an appropriate adverbial to the sentence: *the wind simultaneously . . .* Another possibility is that the speaker is not interested in the relative order of the three events, but is simply registering his observation of the overall result of the wind's damage, in which case he may not even know the actual order of events.

The precise differentiation of tense and aspect is particularly important in considering the perfect,[1] e.g. English *John has read the book* (as

---

[1] In this book the terms 'perfective' and 'perfect' are used in quite different senses from one another; see further section 0.3 below.

opposed to *John read the book*), Spanish *Juan ha leído el libro* (as opposed to *Juan leyó el libro*).¹ This problem is discussed, with references, in chapter 3 on the perfect. Traditionally, in works that make a distinction between tense and aspect, the perfect has usually, but not always, been considered an aspect, although it is doubtful whether the definition of aspect given above can be interpreted to include the perfect as an aspect. However, the perfect is equally not just a tense, since it differs in meaning from the various tense forms.² Since the perfect is very often referred to as an aspect, discussion of it has been included in the present book.³

0.2. **Meaning and form**

So far, aspect has been presented essentially in semantic terms, with reference to the internal structure of a situation, without any discussion of the formal expression of aspect. A brief comparison with tense will be useful here: there is the semantic concept of time reference (absolute or relative), which may be grammaticalised in a language, i.e. a language may have a grammatical category that expresses time reference, in which case we say that the language has tenses. Many languages lack tenses, i.e. do not have grammaticalised time reference, though probably all languages can lexicalise time reference, i.e. have temporal adverbials that locate situations in time, such as English *today, the year before last, at five o'clock*. In treatments of aspect, there is no such uniformity of terminology, so that the term 'aspect' is now used to refer to the general semantic oppositions possible, now restricted to particular grammaticalised oppositions based on these semantic distinctions in individual languages.⁴ In the present book we shall speak

¹ In most of the other Romance languages, at least in their spoken forms, the so-called Perfect (or Compound Past) does not necessarily have perfect meaning, since the opposition as represented in Spanish *leyó* and *ha leído* is lost in favour of the compound form in both meanings. The written languages usually maintain the distinction, e.g. French Perfect *Jean a lu le livre* versus Past Definite (nonperfect) *Jean lut le livre*.
² See further section 3.0.
³ Part of the difficulty seems to stem from a tendency, once aspect has been distinguished from tense, to refer to all verbal categories that are neither tense nor mood as aspect. This use of the term 'aspect' suffers from all the disadvantages that accompanied the earlier use of the term 'tense' as a general cover-term for a variety of different kinds of distinction.
⁴ In addition to the term 'aspect', some linguists also make use of the term 'aktionsart' (plural: aktionsarten): this is a German word meaning 'kinds of action', and although there have been numerous attempts to coin an English equivalent, none of these has become generally accepted. The

of semantic aspectual distinctions, such as that between perfective and imperfective meaning, irrespective of whether they are grammaticalised or lexicalised in individual languages. However the noun 'aspect' will normally, and in the plural 'aspects' always, be restricted to referring to particular grammatical categories in individual languages that correspond in content to the semantic aspectual distinctions drawn. Other solutions to the terminological problem are possible, and will be found in other works on aspect, though once the policy of the present book has been grasped it should not occasion confusion.

Clearly, in any discussion of aspect, preference will be given to examples from languages where aspect exists as a grammatical category, since such languages provide the clearest examples with which to work, even in discussions of the semantic distinctions underlying these grammatical categories. Thus in discussing perfective and imperfective meaning, the easiest examples to work with are from, for instance, Russian and Spanish (in Spanish, in the past tense only), rather than from, say, English, where this particular opposition has not been grammaticalised, and where the particular opposition that has been grammaticalised, namely that between progressive and nonprogressive meaning, is comparable to the imperfective/perfective distinction only in relation to a limited set of verbs (nonstative verbs), and then only if habitual meaning is excluded.[1]

Just as some languages do not grammaticalise time reference to give

distinction between aspect and aktionsart is drawn in at least the following two quite different ways. The first distinction is between aspect as grammaticalisation of the relevant semantic distinctions, while aktionsart represents lexicalisation of the distinctions, irrespective of how these distinctions are lexicalised; this use of aktionsart is similar to the notion of inherent meaning (related to the general semantic definition of aspect given above) discussed in chapter 2. The second distinction, which is that used by most Slavists, and often by scholars in Slavonic countries writing on other languages, is between aspect as grammaticalisation of the semantic distinction, and aktionsart as lexicalisation of the distinction provided that the lexicalisation is by means of derivational morphology. (For a general discussion of derivational morphology, see Matthews (1974: chapter III), where it is referred to as lexical morphology.) This restriction of the use of the term 'aktionsart' in Slavonic linguistics was introduced by Agrell (1908); a comprehensive account of the aktionsarten of Russian, in this sense, is given by Isačenko (1962: 385–418); for Bulgarian, see Ivanova (1974). In view of the confusion that can be caused by these two rather different senses of aktionsart, this term will not be used in the present book.

[1] See further section 1.2.2. on the progressive.

tenses, so some languages do not grammaticalise semantic aspectual distinctions to give aspects. In some forms of German, for instance, namely those where the Simple Past (e.g. *ich ging* 'I went') has been supplanted completely by the Perfect (e.g. *ich bin gegangen* 'I have gone', in these forms of German also 'I went'), there is no grammaticalisation of aspectual distinctions.[1] This does not mean that in these forms of German it is impossible to express the meaning differences that are expressed by means of aspects in those languages that do have aspects. The difference between English *he read the book* and *he was reading the book* can to some extent be captured in German by the difference between *er las das Buch* (which covers the semantic range of both of the English sentences) and *er las im Buch*, literally 'he read in-the book', which has explicitly the meaning of the English Progressive *was reading*. However, this particular way of expressing the semantic difference is not generalisable beyond a very limited set of verbs. In Finnish, the difference between these two sentences can, indeed in this case must, be expressed by a difference in the case of the direct object: in the first sentence the direct object will be in the accusative, i.e. *hän luki kirjan* 'he read the book', while in the second it will be in the partitive, i.e. *hän luki kirjaa* 'he was reading the book'. However, this is not generalisable to all instances: the distinction is completely inapplicable with verbs that do not take a direct object, while in many sentence pairs that do have a direct object the difference between the one with accusative direct object and the one with partitive direct object is not a semantic aspectual distinction at all.[2]

So far, we have not placed any restriction on how semantic aspectual distinctions are to be grammaticalised in order to qualify as aspects, and

---

[1] These forms of German do have distinct Pluperfect and Future Perfect. However, as noted in section 3.0, these forms do not necessarily indicate perfect meaning, but may simply indicate relative past time reference.

[2] The basic meaning of the partitive case in Finnish is that only part of the object referred to is affected by the situation; where a contrast between partitive and non-partitive is possible, the nonpartitive means that the whole of the object is affected. One possible realisation of this distinction is that between perfective and imperfective meaning: since imperfective meaning implies a situation in progress, it equally entails the incomplete affecting of the direct object. However, it is possible for the direct object of a verb with perfective meaning to be only partially affected, as in *hän otti ruokaa* 'he took some food' (cf. *hän otti ruoan* 'he took (all of) the food' with the accusative), or *mies ampui lintua pyrstöön* 'the man shot the bird in the tail', where only part of the bird (its tail) is affected. For details of the partitive in Finnish, see Denison (1957).

indeed we shall not be placing any such additional restrictions, although many other writers on aspect have attempted to do so. Thus aspect as a grammatical category, just like any other grammatical category, may be expressed by means of the inflectional morphology of the language in question, as with Spanish *leyó* and *leía* cited above; it may also be expressed by means of a periphrasis, as with English *he was reading*, the periphrastic Progressive, as opposed to the simple verb form *he read*.[1] Further details of the particular formal devices used to express aspectual oppositions in various languages belong to the grammar of those individual languages, and not to a general book on aspect; in chapter 5, however, certain recurrent parallels among languages in the formal expression of aspectual oppositions will be discussed and interpreted.

In practice, the relation between grammatical categories of individual languages and semantic categories is even more complex than is suggested by the simplistic view of semantic categories that are either grammaticalised or not in particular languages. On the one hand, language-particular categories often combine aspect with some other category, most usually tense. The Spanish Imperfect, for instance, as in *Juan leía* 'Juan was reading, Juan used to read', combines both imperfective meaning and past time reference, i.e. combines both tense and aspect. The same is true of the so-called Perfective in written Arabic (section 4.4), which combines perfective meaning and relative past time reference. On the other hand, one often finds language-particular categories that correspond closely, but not exactly, to semantic distinctions: in section 1.2.2, for instance, we shall see that the English Progressive typically expresses progressive meaning, although its range is in

---

[1] Thus Klein (1974: 76) criticises linguists who consider the English Progressive to be an aspect, since it is a verbal periphrasis. It is, of course, possible to build this restriction into one's definition, but the problem then arises of how to refer to such categories as the English Progressive which are aspectual semantically, are systematically opposed to non-Progressive forms, but are expressed by means of periphrases. There is a more general problem here, which concerns morphology and syntax as a whole rather than just aspect, namely that it is not always easy to draw precise boundaries between derivational (lexical) and inflectional morphology, nor between morphology and syntax (the English Progressive being a case in point). It is usual to consider the French construction *être en train de* 'to be in the process of' as a free syntactic construction that expresses progressive meaning, rather than as a grammatical category of French, although it is not clear exactly where the boundary-line would be drawn between this and the English or Spanish Progressives, which are usually considered as grammatical categories.

fact somewhat wider than is predicted by the general semantic definition of progressive meaning. To avoid confusion between language-particular categories and semantic distinctions defined independently of any particular language, in this book the policy has been adopted of using an initial capital for the names of language-particular categories, whether referring to the category as such or to forms that belong to that category, while not using initial capitals for language-independent semantic distinctions. This typographical convention should be noted carefully in working through the book.

In relating language-particular categories to language-independent semantic characterisations, it is possible, in principle, either to start from the language-particular categories and associate them with their meaning or meanings, or to start from the semantic distinctions and see how, if at all, these are grammaticalised in the individual language (in addition to the possible combination of the two approaches). In a work dealing with aspect from the viewpoint of general linguistics, the second approach, from meaning to form, is the more feasible, since the centre of interest is not the particular forms that exist in any one particular language. In the present work, therefore, various general semantic distinctions are introduced and illustrated by means of language-particular categories that correspond more or less closely to the semantic distinctions established. This does, of course, mean that it will not always be the case that the particular language used to illustrate a general point will have a category that corresponds exactly to the semantic distinction involved – where this does appear to be the case, it is often because not enough work has been done on finer points of usage concerning the language-particular category – but only that there is sufficient overlap to make comparison viable.

It might be thought that the ideal would be to establish for each language-particular category a general characterisation[1] of its meaning such that each one of its individual uses would be predictable from this general characterisation (and, equally, one would be able to predict when not to use the form in question), and there would be no need to speak of only partial correspondence between formal categories and semantic distinctions. To take this as one's starting-point is, of course, to beg the whole question of the degree of complexity of the relation between formal categories and semantic distinctions. An alternative

---

[1] For general meaning, the German term 'gesamtbedeutung' is often found.

approach would be to try and provide the simplest possible characterisation of this relation: in cases where there is a general meaning from which all individual uses are predictable, then this will indeed be the simplest characterisation of the relation, but this approach does not prejudge the question of whether or not there is a single general meaning. In the present work, then, where we speak of a given category having several meanings, the possibility is not excluded that subsequent work may show that these various meanings are in fact different manifestations of one general meaning, or at least of a smaller number of meanings.

Where a form is said to have more than one meaning, it is often the case that one of these meanings seems more central, more typical than the others. In such cases, it is usual to speak of this central meaning as the basic meaning.[1] In certain cases the existence of both basic and secondary meanings can be shown to be the result of a historical process where the basic meaning is the original meaning, while secondary meanings have been acquired as extensions of this original meaning, often leading ultimately to the same form acquiring a new basic meaning much wider than the original basic meaning, and incorporating a number of uses that were originally secondary meanings. One example of this is discussed in section 3.1.4, on the development of the Perfect in many Romance languages to oust the Simple Past, via gradual relaxation of the requirement of present relevance in the use of the Perfect to refer to a past situation. A similar process can be observed in Welsh, for instance, where what was originally a periphrastic form with progressive meaning has gradually extended its domain to encompass almost the whole of imperfective meaning in the present tense, with the exception of only a few stative verbs.

0.3. **Terminology**

As already indicated, in discussions of aspect, as opposed to many other areas of linguistics, there is no generally accepted terminology. The present section will introduce some of the terms used in this book, in particular those where confusion with other terminological systems is especially likely to lead to misunderstanding if the differences between the various terminologies are not appreciated. It should not be thought that all such differences are terminological – in many cases there are also deep-seated conceptual differences – but in a large number of

---

[1] German 'grundbedeutung'; subsidiary meanings are often referred to by the German term 'nebenbedeutungen' (singular 'nebenbedeutung').

instances the difference is purely one of terminology. On the one hand, different labels are often used to refer to the same phenomenon, while on the other hand, and even more confusingly, the same label is often applied by different linguists to radically different concepts.

In this book, the terms 'perfect' and 'perfective' are used in very different senses from one another. The term 'perfective' contrasts with 'imperfective', and denotes a situation viewed in its entirety, without regard to internal temporal constituency; the term 'perfect' refers to a past situation which has present relevance, for instance the present result of a past event (*his arm has been broken*). This terminological distinction is usual in discussions of aspect by Continental linguists, and is insisted on by Slavists, who have to deal with languages like Bulgarian and Old Church Slavonic where both of these oppositions, perfective/imperfective and perfect/nonperfect, are grammaticalised. In many recent works by English-speaking linguists, however, there has been an unfortunate tendency to use the term 'perfective' for what is here termed 'perfect'; this tendency is particularly unfortunate when it leads to conceptual confusion, such as the view that what Slavists call perfective is the same as perfect in, say, English. In place of the term 'perfective' some linguists use the term 'aoristic'; in the traditional grammatical terminologies of some languages, however, the term 'aorist' is restricted to perfectivity in the past tense (e.g. Bulgarian, Georgian, also some writers on Spanish), and to avoid this possible confusion the term has not been used as part of the general linguistic terminology here.[1]

In the discussion of subdivisions of imperfectivity, a distinction is made between the terms 'progressive' and 'continuous', the former being a subdivision of the latter (progressiveness is the combination of continuousness with nonstativity). In traditional discussions of English, the forms here referred to as Progressive (e.g. *John was reading*) are sometimes referred to as continuous, so the particular distinction made here between the two terms should be carefully noted.

In the discussion of language-particular categories, the traditional names of these categories in the grammar of the language concerned have usually been retained. This has meant in certain cases using different terms for language-particular categories expressing more or less the

---

[1] In Ancient Greek, the Aorist is in the Indicative Mood primarily a past tense, although it does have some nonpast uses. In other moods and in nonfinite forms, the Aorist is purely aspectual, not an expression of tense.

same semantic distinctions (such as Aorist, Past Definite, for perfective past, in Bulgarian and written French respectively), and, rather less felicitously, using traditional terms that do not correspond to the general linguistic terminology used in this book (e.g. the Latin Perfect, which is a perfective past, and does not distinguish perfect/nonperfect meaning;[1] the Arabic Perfective, which is a perfective relative past, although the term seems to refer only to its aspectual value).[2] Careful observation of the use of initial capitals should prevent any confusion.

In discussing aspect, it is often necessary to refer to the differences between states, events, processes, etc.; these are discussed more fully in chapter 2. However, while ordinary nontechnical language provides, with a limited amount of systematisation, a metalanguage for these various subdivisions, it does not provide any general term to subsume them all. In the present work the term 'situation' is used as this general cover-term, i.e. a situation may be either a state, or an event, or a process. The use of the terms 'state', 'event', 'process' is discussed in further detail in section 2.3. For the present, we may take the distinction as follows: states are static, i.e. continue as before unless changed, whereas events and processes are dynamic, i.e. require a continual input of energy if they are not to come to an end; events are dynamic situations viewed as a complete whole (perfectively), whereas processes are dynamic situations viewed in progress, from within (imperfectively).

0.4. **Structure of the book**

A brief outline of the structure of the book will enable the reader to find his way more easily about the book as a whole.

The core of the book is formed by chapters 1 to 3, in which the major concepts utilised in the study of aspect are introduced and discussed. Chapter 1 discusses in greater detail the distinctions between perfective and imperfective, already outlined in section 0.1; it also discusses briefly some of the misleading characterisations of this distinction that appear in the literature, in particular the earlier literature, although some of these can still be found in more recent work. This chapter then goes on to discuss various subdivisions of imperfectivity, in particular habituality, continuousness, and progressiveness. The interaction of different aspectual categories with one another in a variety of languages is also discussed and illustrated.

[1] E.g. *necavi* 'I killed', or 'I have killed'.
[2] See further section 4.4.

Chapter 2 looks at how the inherent meaning of certain lexical items and syntactic combinations of lexical items can determine semantic aspectual characteristics, and how these in turn interact with the aspectual categories of individual languages. Distinctions discussed include that between state and dynamic situation, that between durative and punctual situations, that between being in a state or process, entering a state or process, and leaving a state of process, and that between situations which move towards a logical conclusion (telic) and those that do not.

The perfect is discussed in chapter 3, which gives examples of various kinds of perfect all consistent with the general characterisation of perfectness as the present relevance of a prior situation.

Chapters 4 and 5 use the conceptual background provided by the earlier chapters. Chapter 4 investigates the interaction of aspect and tense in various languages, and also aspect and voice. In chapter 5, formal means of expressing aspect are discussed where the particular formal devices used are closely linked to the semantic distinction expressed, and thus provide a window onto the semantic distinctions.

Chapter 6 discusses the concept of markedness as applied to aspectual oppositions, both in the sense in which it is used by adherents of the Prague School, and in the somewhat wider sense it has gained in more recent linguistic literature.

Finally, two appendices give a genetic classification of the languages cited in the book with brief characterisations of the aspectual systems of some of the languages that play a major role in the presentation of data in the body of the book, and introduce the reader briefly to three recent approaches to the analysis of aspect.

0.5. General reading

There are relatively few works on aspect from the viewpoint of general linguistics, rather than in individual languages; references to works on individual languages will be found in appendix A, and in the list of references at the end of the book. An influential general work is Holt (1943), with emphasis on Slavonic and Ancient Greek material.

Two readers which reprint a number of articles, both theoretical and descriptive, are Maslov (1962a) and Schopf (1974a). All the articles in Maslov (1962a), and the editor's introduction (Maslov 1962b) are reprinted in Russian. Those in Schopf (1974a) are reprinted in English or German; the editor's introductory sections are in German. Although this latter reader deals primarily with the English Progressive, it also contains a number of introductory articles on aspect from a general linguistic viewpoint, and has a comprehensive bibliography of general works on aspect.

For an early critique of the tendency to classify various heterogeneous distinctions as aspect, see Jespersen (1924:286–9),[1] though with a rather different terminology from that in most later works.

---

[1] Although Jespersen heads this section 'Aspect', he says: 'I do not give the following system as representing various "aspects" or "aktionsarten" of the verb, but expressly say that the different phenomena which others have brought together under this one class (or these two classes) should not from a purely notional point of view be classed together' (p. 287).

I

Perfective and imperfective

1.0. The distinction between perfectivity and imperfectivity has already been outlined, in section 0.1: perfectivity indicates the view of a situation as a single whole, without distinction of the various separate phases that make up that situation; while the imperfective pays essential attention to the internal structure of the situation. The present chapter will look at this distinction in further detail, with examples drawn from various languages.

1.1. **Perfective**

1.1.1. *Definition of perfectivity*

Before illustrating in more detail what is meant by perfectivity, it may be worth discussing briefly some frequently cited, but essentially inadequate characterisations of this notion: many of these are quite widespread in the general linguistic literature on aspect and in grammars of individual languages, and lead frequently to incorrect assessments of the role of aspect.[1]

It is sometimes claimed that perfective forms indicate situations of short duration, while imperfective forms indicate situations of long duration. It is easy to find examples from individual languages that contradict this assertion, perhaps the clearest being where both perfective and imperfective forms can be used in referring to the same length of time, without any necessary implication of the duration being

---

[1] Since we are not concerned with the history of theories of aspect, except incidentally, detailed references have not been given for each of the various characterisations discussed below. A first-rate summary of the historical development of accounts of perfectivity (and imperfectivity), with particular regard to Slavonic, is given by Dostál (1954: 10–18). Some of these earlier accounts, in particular those from the nineteenth century, though shown to be inadequate by later work, still played an important role in the development of the study of aspect.

short or long. Thus in Russian, *I stood there for an hour* can be translated either in the Imperfective, *ja stojal tam čas*, or in at least the following two perfective forms: *ja postojal tam čas, ja prostojal tam čas*. To the extent that any of these give any indication of whether the period of standing was long or short, it is the first Perfective version (with *postojal*) that suggests a (subjectively) short period, and the second Perfective version (with *prostojal*) that suggests a (subjectively) long period, while the Imperfective (*stojal*) is quite neutral. Similarly, in French the difference between *il régna* (Past Definite) *trente ans* and *il régnait* (Imperfect) *trente ans* 'he reigned for thirty years' is not one of objective or subjective difference in the period of the reign; rather the former gathers the whole period of thirty years into a single complete whole, corresponding roughly to the English 'he had a reign of thirty years', i.e. one single reign, while the second says rather that at any point during those thirty years he was indeed reigning, i.e. is connected more with the internal structuring of the reign, and would be more appropriate as a background statement to a discussion of the individual events that occurred during his reign. Similarly in Ancient Greek, we find the Aorist (perfective past) in *ebasíleuse déka étē* 'he reigned ten years', or rather 'he had a reign of ten years', to bring out the difference between this form and the Imperfect (imperfective past) *ebasíleue déka étē* 'he reigned for ten years', or more explicitly 'he was reigning during ten years'.

Equally, the perfective cannot be defined as describing a situation with limited, as opposed to unlimited, duration; an hour, ten years, thirty years, are all limited periods, but as the examples above show both perfective and imperfective forms can be used to describe such duration.

Related to the concept of perfectivity as indicating a short period of time is its characterisation as indicating a punctual (i.e. point-like) or momentary situation. Examples such as those discussed above serve to disconfirm this view of perfectivity, since in each case they refer to a situation extending over a (long) period of time, and are not used specifically for momentary situations of the type 'give a cough', 'give a slap'.[1] While it is incorrect to say that the basic function of the perfective is to represent an event as momentary or punctual, there is some truth in the view that the perfective, by not giving direct expression to the internal structure of a situation, irrespective of its objective

[1] See further section 2.1.

complexity, has the effect of reducing it to a single point. In section 1.1.2, however, we shall see that perfectivity can be combined with certain other aspectual properties, in accordance with the general morphological and syntactic properties of the individual language, and that this yields perfective forms that are clearly not punctual, such as Russian *on pozapiral vse dveri* 'he locked each of the doors individually, locked them one after the other': the element 'each', 'individually', or 'one after the other' is essential to an adequate rendering in English of *pozapiral*, which contrasts with another Perfective form *zaper*, which would also cover the possibility of simultaneous locking of all the doors. Since the notion of a point seems to preclude internal complexity, a more helpful metaphor would perhaps be to say that the perfective reduces a situation to a blob, rather than to a point: a blob is a three-dimensional object, and can therefore have internal complexity, although it is nonetheless a single object with clearly circumscribed limits.

A very frequent characterisation of perfectivity is that it indicates a completed action. One should note that the word at issue in this definition is 'completed', not 'complete': despite the formal similarity between the two words, there is an important semantic distinction which turns out to be crucial in discussing aspect. The perfective does indeed denote a complete situation, with beginning, middle, and end. The use of 'completed', however, puts too much emphasis on the termination of the situation, whereas the use of the perfective puts no more emphasis, necessarily, on the end of a situation than on any other part of the situation, rather all parts of the situation are presented as a single whole.[1] The existence of a Perfective Future in Russian, for instance, e.g. *ja ub'ju tebja* 'I shall kill you', and of subordinate perfective forms with (relative) future time reference in Ancient Greek, for instance, e.g. *boúletai toũto poiẽsai* 'he wishes to do this', with the Aorist Infinitive, further demonstrates the inadequacy of 'completed', rather than 'complete', as a characterisation of the perfective.[2] In Russian, some

---

[1] The confusion has been partly fostered by the terminology of many grammatical traditions, e.g. Czech *dokonavý*, Polish *dokonany*, Latin *perfectivum*, all of which derive from verbs meaning 'to complete'.

[2] Interestingly enough, the so-called Perfective in Arabic, which is also often defined as indicating a completed situation, is not the form used for future time reference, even for situations viewed as complete; see further section 4.4.

verbs do have derivationally related forms that indicate specifically the completion of a situation: thus alongside *užinat'* (Ipfv.) 'have supper' there is *otužinat'* 'finish supper', as in *my tol'ko čto otužinali* 'we've just finished supper'; however, this verb is distinct from the Perfective of *užinat'*, which is *použinat'*, as in *my použinali posle polunoči* 'we had supper after midnight', referring to the whole of the meal, not just its end. Indicating the end of a situation is at best only one of the possible meanings of a perfective form, certainly not its defining feature. A perfective form often indicates the completion of a situation when it is explicitly contrasted with an imperfective form: since the imperfective indicates a situation in progress, and since the perfective indicates a situation which has an end, the only new semantic element introduced by the perfective is that of the termination of the situation, as in Russian *on dolgo ugovarival* (Ipfv.) *menja, no ne ugovoril* (Pfv.) 'he persuaded (Ipfv.) me for a long time, but didn't persuade (Pfv.) me', i.e. 'he spent a long time trying to persuade me, but didn't actually persuade me'.

In many languages that have a distinction between perfective and imperfective forms, the perfective forms of some verbs, in particular of some stative verbs, can in fact be used to indicate the beginning of a situation (ingressive meaning). In Ancient Greek, for instance, the Aorist (perfective past) of the verb *basileúō* 'I reign' can refer to a complete reign, as in *ebasíleusa déka étē* 'I reigned for ten years, had a reign of ten years', but it can also refer to the start of the reign, i.e. *ebasíleusa* 'I became king, ascended the throne' versus Imperfect (imperfective past) *ebasíleuon* 'I was king'. Similarly with the verb *sunoikéō* 'I cohabit', as in *allà parà zõntos Timokrátous ekeínōi sunōíkēse* (Aorist) 'but leaving Timocrates, who was still alive, she went to live with him'.[1] A similar situation obtains in Spanish with, for instance, the verbs *ver* 'see', *conocer* 'know' (i.e. 'be acquainted with'), *saber* 'know' (for instance, know a fact): the Simple Past (perfective past) of these verbs often indicates the start of a new situation, as in *conocí* (Simple Past) *a Pedro hace muchos años* 'I got to know Pedro many years ago'. In Russian, *ponjat'*, the Perfective of *ponimat'* 'understand', usually has the meaning 'come to understand, grasp', as in *nakonec on ponjal, v čem delo* 'at last he grasped what was up'.[2] In Mandarin Chinese, too,

---

[1] The Ancient Greek examples are from Goodwin (1889: 16).

[2] In Russian, given the way in which aspect is expressed morphologically (see section 5.1.1), it is often difficult to decide whether semantically similar Perfective and Imperfective forms are in fact different aspectual

a number of predicates, both adjectives and verbs, that normally refer to a state can have ingressive meaning in the Perfective, e.g. *tā gāo* 'he is tall', *tā gāo-le* (Pfv.) 'he became tall, has become tall'.[1] Clearly, one cannot say that such perfective forms indicate the completion of a situation, when in fact they refer to its inception.

A possible analysis of this ingressive meaning would be to say that such verbs can in general be either stative or ingressive, i.e. can in general refer either to the state or to entry into that state, like, for instance, English *sit* (which can mean either 'be sitting' or 'adopt a sitting position'); compare also English *and suddenly he knew/understood what was happening*, where the meaning is also ingressive. One could further claim that the choice between ingressive and stative interpretation is determined by the context, rather than by any special proviso that such perfective forms can have ingressive meaning. Whether this claim can be maintained is, however, doubtful, since there is a crucial difference between *sit*, for instance, on the one hand, and the other verbs listed here: *sit* can be used in all forms with the meaning 'adopt a sitting posture', including forms with imperfective meaning, e.g. the Progressive *he is just sitting down*. One cannot, however, use *know* in this way (**he's knowing what's happening*), nor the similar forms from the other languages. *Know* thus differs from *realise*, which refers explicitly to entry into a new situation, and can be used in the Progressive (*he's slowly realising what's happening*). There may be some sense in saying that since states are less likely to be described by perfective forms than are events (including entries into states), then there is some functional value in utilising the perfective forms of stative verbs to denote the event of entry into the appropriate state, since otherwise there would be little use for the perfective forms of these verbs, but such an explanation is at present speculative.

Similar to the definition of the perfective in terms of a completed action is its definition as being a resultative, i.e. indicating the successful completion of a situation. It is true that perfective forms of certain individual verbs do effectively indicate the successful completion of a situation, as with Russian *ja ugovoril* (Pfv.) *ego* versus *ja ugovarival* (Ipfv.) *ego*, which could be rendered into English as 'I succeeded in

forms of the same verb, or different verbs, albeit related in the derivational morphology. In the case of *ponimat'/ponjat'*, other verbs of this rare morphological pattern are aspectual pairs (e.g. *nanimat'/nanjat'* 'hire', *zanimat'/zanjat'* 'occupy'), suggesting that *ponimat'/ponjat'* is too.

[1] Cp. Jaxontov (1957: 116).

persuading him' and 'I tried to persuade him'.[1] But resultativity is only one possible type of perfectivity, and the term 'resultative', like the term 'completed', puts unnecessary emphasis on the final stage of the situation rather than on its totality. Again, usages like Spanish *supe* 'I realised, came to know', from *saber* 'know', contradict the view that perfectivity indicates successful completion: whatever the event referred to by *supe* is the successful outcome of, it is not the situation referred to by *sabía* 'I knew'; if anything, the reverse is true, with the situation referred to by the imperfective *sabía* being the result of the event referred to by *supe*.

Finally, we may consider the view that the perfective represents the action pure and simple, without any additional overtones. In effect, this claims that perfectives are the unmarked members of any aspectual opposition based on perfectivity; we shall return to the question of markedness with relation to aspectual oppositions later (chapter 6), but for the moment it will suffice to note that there are both languages where a perfective is marked (e.g. the Perfective in the Slavonic languages), and languages where a perfective is unmarked (e.g. the Past Definite in French, the Aorist in Ancient Greek, Bulgarian, and Georgian). Thus this attempted definition does not give a language-independent definition of perfectivity, and even in those languages where it does identify the perfective this is not because of the inherent meaning of the perfective, but rather because of the functioning of the perfective as the unmarked member of the binary opposition perfective/imperfective.

1.1.2. *Perfectivity and other aspectual values*

From the definition of perfectivity given above, it follows that perfectivity involves lack of explicit reference to the internal temporal constituency of a situation, rather than explicitly implying the lack of such internal temporal constituency. Thus it is quite possible for perfective forms to be used for situations that are internally complex, such as those that last for a considerable period of time, or include a number of distinct internal phases, provided only that the whole of the situation is subsumed as a single whole. Clearly the internal structure of such situations cannot be referred to directly by the choice of a perfective form, since this is precisely what perfective forms cannot indicate, but such reference can be made explicitly by other means, such as the

[1] See further section 2.2.

lexical meáning of the verb involved, or other aspectual oppositions, or other facets of the context. The present section will look at various examples which illustrate this phenomenon more clearly.

As already noted, perfectivity is by no means incompatible with overt expression of the duration of a situation, as in the following examples, repeated for convenience, all of which contain perfective verb forms: French *il régna trente ans,* Ancient Greek *ebasíleuse déka étē* 'he reigned thirty years', Russian *on postojal/prostojal tam čas* 'he stood there for an hour'.[1] To this list we might add Mandarin Chinese *bàgōng jìxù-le* (Pfv.) *wŭ tiān* 'the strike lasted for five days'.[2] The Russian examples are particularly interesting here in that the sole function of the perfectivising prefixes *po-* and *pro-* with verbs of this class is to indicate a temporally restricted, but nonpunctual, situation;[3] i.e. here it is the lexical meaning of the verb in *po-* or *pro-* that explicitly expresses duration.

In Spanish, in the past tense, the opposition Simple Past versus Imperfect can be expressed independently of the opposition Progressive versus non-Progressive, the former by the form of the finite verb, the latter by the use or non-use of the construction *estar* plus Present Participle. In principle, then, one might expect, on structural grounds, the form Aorist of *estar* plus Present Participle, i.e. in effect a perfective progressive, such as *estuvieron entrando* 'they entered, were entering'. And in practice such forms do occur, albeit rarely, as in *toda la tarde estuvieron entrando visitas* 'all the afternoon visitors kept arriving'.[4]

---

[1] In Russian, there is a clear test to tell whether a verb is Perfective or Imperfective. Imperfective verbs have a Future Tense distinct from the Present Tense, and formed with the auxiliary *budu* plus the Infinitive; Perfective verbs have only one non-Past Tense, and cannot be used with *budu.* (For the time reference of the Perfective non-Past, see section 4.1.) The simple verb *stojat'* has Present *ja stoju* 'I stand, am standing', and Future *ja budu stojat'* 'I shall stand, shall be standing'. The prefixed verbs *postojat'* and *prostojat'* have only one non-Past, normally with future meaning, i.e. *ja postoju* 'I shall stand for a while', *ja prostoju (čas)* 'I shall stand (for all of an hour)'; there is no **ja budu postojat'* or **ja budu prostojat'.* Thus *stojat'* is Imperfective, while *postojat'* and *prostojat'* are both Perfective.

[2] Jaxontov (1957: 117).

[3] See further Isačenko (1962: 391–3, 394), who uses the terms 'delimitative' for such verbs in *po-*, and the term 'perdurative' for such verbs in *pro-*.

[4] This example is quoted by Stevenson (1970: 63), with the comment 'the action, though viewed as continuous or continuing in time, is also regarded as a complete whole'.

The situation described is one that lasted through time (in fact, the whole of the afternoon), and consists of a number of distinct phases (the various arrivals), whence the Progressive; however, the whole complex is equally presented as a single complete whole, whence the Simple Past. Similar usages are found in Portuguese, e.g. *ele esteve lendo em casa o dia inteiro* 'he spent the whole day at home reading'.[1]

In Bulgarian, again in the past tense, there are two morphological oppositions corresponding to the perfective versus nonperfective distinction, namely that between Perfective and Imperfective, and that between Aorist and Imperfect. One of the main uses of the apparently self-contradictory Imperfective Aorist is precisely to indicate an action which is presented as a single whole (whence the Aorist as marker of perfectivity), but with internal complexity (whence the Imperfective as marker of imperfectivity), as in the following example:[2] *pred mnogi ikoni ošte pop Stefan vodi* (Ipfv. Aorist) *djada Nedka. Te se spiraxa* (Ipfv. Aorist) *pred sv. Nikolaj Čudotvorec, . . ., pred obrazite na arxangelite Gavrail i Mixail . . .* 'Father Stephen led (Ipfv. Aorist) old Nedko in front of many other icons. They stopped (Ipfv. Aorist) before St. Nicholas the Thaumaturge, . . ., before the images of the archangels Gabriel and Michael . . .'

Russian, with its less profuse aspectual morphology, is not normally able to give direct expression to a single whole with internal structuring: either the situation is presented as a single whole (Perfective), or it is unfolded into its component parts (Imperfective). However, where internal structuring can be indicated other than by the Perfective/Imperfective opposition, then Russian too can directly express situations viewed in the way we have been discussing. With the Perfective *zaperet'* 'lock', we can have sentences like *on zaper dver'* 'he locked the door', *on zaper vse dveri* 'he locked all the doors'; the latter simply informs us that he locked all the doors, without giving any indication as to how (in what order, or perhaps all at once by pushing a control-button) the doors were locked. But there is also the derivationally related

---

[1] Thomas (1969: 202). *Esteve lendo* is literally 'was (Simple Past) reading'; in English the force of both Simple Past and Progressive can be brought out by factoring out the Simple Past *spent* and the Progressive form *reading*. A similar combination of aspects is possible in English with constructions of the type: *it happened* (perfective) *one day that I was walking* (imperfective) *along the street . . .*, *I happened one day to be walking along the street . . .*

[2] Andrejczin (1938: 39).

Perfective verb *pozapirat'*, as in *on pozapiral vse dveri*, which specifies that the doors were locked individually, one after the other:[1] although the Perfective Aspect still views the situation as a single complete whole, the distributive lexical meaning of this verb gives information as to the internal constituency of this action. Compare also *vse povskakali so svoix mest* 'they all jumped up from their seats (one after the other)' versus *vse vskočili so svoix mest* 'they all jumped up from their seats (possibly all together)'.

The same phenomenon obtains with a Russian verb like *pereklikat'sja* (Ipfv.)/*perekliknut'* (Pfv.) 'call to one another', which refers to a sequential interchange of calls; cp. also *peremigivat'sja* (Ipfv.)/*peremignut'sja* (Pfv.) 'wink at one another', i.e. a sequential interchange of winks.[2] With the Perfective in a sentence like *deti perekliknulis'* 'the children called to one another', the internal phases of the situation are referred to by the lexical meaning of the verb, while the Perfective draws them together as a single whole. As a final Russian example, we may consider *posetiteli ponanesli grjazi v komnatu* 'little by little, the visitors brought lots of mud into the room'.[3] The Perfective *ponanesli* here indicates a gradual process whereby each of the visitors brought some mud into the room until a stage was reached where a considerable amount of mud had been accumulated in the room. This may be contrasted with the semantically more neutral *posetiteli prinesli grjaz' v komnatu* 'the visitors brought mud into the room'.

1.2. Imperfective

1.2.0. From the above discussion, the general characterisation of imperfectivity will already be apparent, namely explicit reference to the internal temporal structure of a situation, viewing a situation from within; as also will be the general point that imperfectivity is not incompatible with perfectivity, and that both can be expressed if the language in question possesses the formal means to do so, as in the examples quoted in section 1.1.2.

While many languages do have a single category to express imperfectivity, there are other languages where imperfectivity is subdivided into a number of distinct categories, and yet others where there is some

---

[1] See further Isačenko (1962: 409–14), who uses the term 'distributive' for such verbs.

[2] Isačenko (1962: 409), who uses the term 'mutual'.

[3] Isačenko (1962: 395), who uses the term 'cumulative-distributive'.

category that corresponds to part only of the meaning of imperfectivity. To jump ahead somewhat, we may represent the most typical sub-divisions of imperfectivity as in table 1.

Table 1. *Classification of aspectual oppositions*

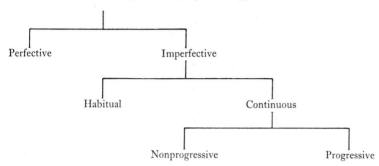

We may look briefly at some languages which have aspects expressing different groupings of these semantic distinctions. English, for instance, has a separate Habitual Aspect, though only in the past tense, e.g. *John used to work here*; there is also a separate Progressive, e.g. *John was working (when I entered)*; otherwise there is just the Simple form, with no further distinction of aspect, indeed given the optionality of the Habitual Aspect in English a sentence like *John worked here* may have habitual meaning, the only excluded possibility being progressive meaning. In the past tense Spanish, however, has a straight distinction between perfective and imperfective, in the Simple Past/Imperfect distinction, e.g. *Juan llegó* (Simple Past) 'John arrived' versus *Juan llegaba* (Imperfect) 'John was arriving, John used to arrive'; there is a separate Progressive form, *Juan estaba llegando* 'John was arriving', although this form is optional, since *Juan llegaba* does not exclude progressive meaning. In Welsh, different dialects have different systems in the past tense, although the existence of a Simple Past with perfective meaning is common to all dialects, e.g. *darllenais i 'Y Faner'* 'I read *The Banner*'. In South Welsh this contrasts with the one, periphrastic, form *yr oeddwn i yn darllen 'Y Faner'* 'I was reading *The Banner*' or 'I used to read *The Banner*'. In North Welsh, however, the form *yr oeddwn i yn darllen 'Y Faner'* is nonhabitual, i.e. 'I was reading *The Banner*', whereas there is a separate habitual form, the so-called Imperfect, e.g. *darllenwn i 'Y Faner'* 'I used to read *The Banner*'. In Lithuanian, too, the so-called Imperfect indicates habituality, e.g.

atsikeldavau anksti 'I used to get up early'; thus *bĕgdavau* (Imperfect) 'I used to run' contrasts with the other past tense *bĕgau* 'I ran, I was running'. The following languages all have a general imperfective form, which thus corresponds to both Habitual and Progressive (as well as non-Progressive forms that do not have perfective meaning) in English; all the sentences may be glossed as 'he was reading, used to read *Le Monde, Pravda, Rabotničesko delo, Tà Néa, Brdzola*': French *il lisait* (Imperfect) '*Le Monde*'; Russian *on čital* (Ipfv.) '*Pravdu*'; Bulgarian *četeše* (Ipfv. Imperfect) '*Rabotničesko delo*'; Modern Greek *diávaze* (Ipfv. Past) '*Tà Néa*'; Georgian *is ķitxulobda* (Ipfv. Imperfect) '*Brʒolas*'.

In traditional grammars of many languages with a category covering the whole of imperfectivity, the impression is given that the general area of imperfectivity must be subdivided into two quite distinct concepts of habituality and continuousness.[1] Thus one is told that the imperfective form expresses either a habitual situation or a situation viewed in its duration, and the term 'imperfective' is glossed as 'continuous-habitual' (or 'durative-habitual'). This approach, unlike that adopted in the present book, fails to recognise that these various subdivisions do in fact join together to form a single unified concept, as is suggested by the large number of languages that have a single category to express imperfectivity as a whole, irrespective of such subdivisions as habituality and continuousness.

In discussing perfectivity, we noted that it is possible to use perfective forms to refer to situations that have internal structure. From the definition of imperfectivity, however, it follows that imperfective forms cannot be used to refer to situations lacking internal structure. The question that remains is whether or not there are any situations that are strictly punctual, in the sense that they cannot be viewed as lasting in time, as consisting of several successive phases. We shall return to this question in section 2.1.

1.2.1. *Habitual*

1.2.1.0. In discussing habituality and continuousness, it is easiest to start by giving a positive definition of habituality, leaving continuousness to be defined negatively as imperfectivity that is not habituality. Most of this section will, therefore, be concerned with the definition of habituality.

---

[1] In other terminologies, durativity.

In some discussions of habituality, it is assumed that habituality is essentially the same as iterativity, i.e. the repetition of a situation, the successive occurrence of several instances of the given situation.[1] This terminology is misleading in two senses. Firstly, the mere repetition of a situation is not sufficient for that situation to be referred to by a specifically habitual (or, indeed, imperfective) form. If a situation is repeated a limited number of times, then all of these instances of the situation can be viewed as a single situation, albeit with internal structure, and referred to by a perfective form. Imagine, for instance, a scene where a lecturer stands up, coughs five times, and then goes on to deliver his lecture. In English, this could be described as follows: *the lecturer stood up, coughed five times, and said* . . . It would not be possible to use the specifically habitual form with *used to*, i.e. not **the lecturer stood up, used to cough five times, and said* . . . In French, similarly, one could express this by using the perfective Past Definite throughout: *le conférencier se leva, toussa cinq fois, et dit* . . . Russian too can use the Perfective here:[2] *dokladčik vstal, kašljanul pjat' raz i skazal* . . . Secondly, a situation can be referred to by a habitual form without there being any iterativity at all. In a sentence like *the Temple of Diana used to stand at Ephesus*, there is no necessary implication that there were several occasions on each of which this temple stood at Ephesus, with intervening periods when it did not; with this particular sentence, the natural interpretation is precisely that the temple stood at Ephesus throughout a certain single period, without intermission. The same is true of the following sentences: *Simon used to believe in ghosts, Jones used to live in Patagonia*, and of the Russian sentence *ja ego znaval* 'I used to know him'.

Having clarified the difference between habituality and iterativity, we may now turn to the definition of habituality itself. The feature that is common to all habituals, whether or not they are also iterative, is that they describe a situation which is characteristic of an extended

---

[1] In Slavonic linguistics, habitual forms are often referred to by the term 'iterative' (Russian *mnogokratnyj*), e.g. Russian *pivat'*, *znavat'*, the habitual counterparts of *pit'* 'drink', *znat'* 'know'. (In Russian, as opposed to some other Slavonic languages (e.g. Czech), special habitual forms are used rarely, at least in the written language (Isačenko 1962: 405–7); they can always be replaced by the nonhabitual Imperfective.) In Lithuanian, the Imperfect is called *būtasis dažninis laikas*, i.e. 'past iterative tense'.

[2] Despite the traditional terminology, which refers to *kašljanut'* 'cough' as semelfactive (Latin *semel* 'once').

period of time, so extended in fact that the situation referred to is viewed not as an incidental property of the moment but, precisely, as a characteristic feature of a whole period. If the individual situation is one that can be protracted indefinitely in time, then there is no need for iterativity to be involved (as in *the Temple of Diana used to stand at Ephesus*), though equally it is not excluded (as in *the policeman used to stand at the corner for two hours each day*). If the situation is one that cannot be protracted, then the only reasonable interpretation will involve iterativity (as in *the old professor used always to arrive late*).

The problem of just what constitutes a characteristic feature of an extended period of time, rather than an accidental situation, is conceptual, rather than linguistic, as can be illustrated using the example *Sally used to throw stones at my window in the morning*; clearly if she threw stones two or three times only, the sentence is inappropriate, while it is appropriate if over a period of several years she threw stones at my window every morning; but between these two extremes, it is more difficult to determine precisely how often, and with what degree of regularity (for surely a few mornings could pass without the stones), Sally would have to throw stones to make this an appropriate utterance. In other words, once we have decided that something constitutes a characteristic situation, we are free to use an explicitly habitual form to describe it, but the decision that a situation is characteristic is not in itself linguistic.

In discussions of the English Habitual Past (e.g. *I used to sit for hours on end at their place*), and likewise of the Russian Habitual Past (e.g. *ja u nix sižival celymi časami*),[1] it is often claimed that a further element of the meaning of these forms is that the situation described no longer holds, i.e. that, in the example quoted, I no longer sit for hours at their place. Thus it would be an implication of the sentence *Bill used to belong to a subversive organisation* that Bill no longer belongs to a subversive organisation. If this were an implication in the strict sense, then clearly any addition to the sentence that contradicted this implication would produce a contradiction. It is clearly an implication of *Bill used to belong to a subversive organisation* that Bill has at some time or other belonged to a subversive organisation, so that if someone says that Bill used to belong to a subversive organisation, but that he has

---

[1] Cp. Isačenko (1962: 407), where *ja ego znaval* and its English translation *I used to know him* are said to imply that I no longer know him.

never belonged to a subversive organisation, then he is evidently contradicting himself. We may therefore ask whether the putative implication of the Habitual Past, namely that the situation described no longer holds, is an implication in the strict sense. In fact, it turns out not to be, since one can quite reasonably say, without self-contradiction, in answer to a question whether or not Bill used to be a member of a subversive organisation: *yes, he used to be a member of a subversive organisation, and he still is.* Equally, one could answer: *he used to be . . ., but I don't know whether or not he is now* (as opposed to **he used to be, but I don't know whether he ever has been*). Equally, one could answer: *he used to be, but is no longer a member,* without being unduly repetitive (as opposed to *he used to be, and has at some time been a member of a subversive organisation,* which is repetitive, and odd in that the second clause makes a weaker claim than the first one). Thus this cannot be an implication in the strict sense, since the putative implication can be cancelled by an explicit denial of it.

Suppose, however, that in reply to the question whether or not Bill used to be a member of a subversive organisation I answer simply *yes,* or *yes, he used to be.* Suppose moreover that I know that Bill still is a member of such an organisation. Then the questioner, once he were to discover that I had all this knowledge, could well accuse me of being misleading, if not of outright lying. In the absence of any disclaimer to the contrary, the sentence *Bill used to be a member of a subversive organisation* will be taken by the hearer as a commitment on the speaker's part that Bill is no longer a member. If Bill is still a member, indeed even if the speaker is simply unsure whether or not Bill is still a member, then the hearer can reasonably expect of the speaker that he will add some such disclaimer, otherwise the speaker is being deliberately misleading. In recent linguistic work, the proposition *Bill is no longer a member of a subversive organisation* is often described as an implicature, rather than an implication, of *Bill used to be a member of a subversive organisation.* An implicature is thus weaker than an implication: an implicature of a sentence can be denied, in which case it does not hold, but if not denied, or suspended by an explicit remark from the speaker to the effect that he does not know whether or not it holds, then it will be taken to hold.[1] With this English example one can compare the following Russian example, where again the implicature of the Habitual Past *sišivala* is cancelled by the following remark: *ty, Veronika, často*

---

[1] Cp. Grice (1975).

zdes' sišivala – tut i ostaneš'sja 'you often used to sit here, Veronika, so you can just stay here'.[1]

1.2.1.1. Habitual and other aspectual values

Since any situation that can be protracted sufficiently in time, or that can be iterated a sufficient number of times over a long enough period – and this means, in effect, almost any situation – can be expressed as a habitual, it follows that habituality is in principle combinable with various other semantic aspectual values, namely those appropriate to the kind of situation that is prolonged or iterated. If the formal structure of the language permits combination of the overt markers of these various semantic aspectual values, then we can have forms that give overt expression both to habituality and to some other aspectual value.

In English, for instance, the Habitual Aspect (*used to* construction) can combine freely with Progressive Aspect, to give such forms as *used to be playing*. Since progressiveness has not yet been dealt with in detail we may restrict ourselves for the moment to the following type of contrast between Progressive and non-Progressive, taking initially sentences in the Future Tense, where there is no special habitual form: (a) *when I visit John, he'll recite his latest poems*; (b) *when I visit John, he'll be reciting his latest poems*. In the (a) sentence, with the non-Progressive verb *will recite* in the main clause, the implication is that John's recital will occur after my arrival at his house, whereas in the (b) sentence the implication is that his recital will have started before my arrival, and will continue for at least part of the time that I am there. In this case, then, the Progressive indicates a situation (John's reciting his latest poems) that frames another situation (my arrival), while the non-Progressive excludes this interpretation. If we now put these same sentences into the Habitual Aspect, then precisely the same difference between Progressive and non-Progressive remains: (a) *when I visited John, he used to recite his latest poems*, indicating that on each occasion I went to John's, and only then did the poetry recital start, versus (b) *when I visited John, he used to be reciting his latest poems*, which implies that on each occasion I visited John and he was already engaged in reciting his poetry.[2]

---

[1] This example is from Forsyth (1970: 169).

[2] It is equally possible to use the Habitual in the subordinate clause, of course: *when I used to visit John, he used to recite/be reciting his latest poems*. In English, the expression of habituality is always optional, since the nonhabitual forms do not exclude habituality

In cases like this, where habituality does involve iterativity, then by combining habituality with other aspectual values it is possible to specify the aspectual nature of each individual occurrence of the situations which go together to make up the characteristic situation referred to by the habitual form. In Russian, for instance, particularly where the rest of the context indicates habituality, it is possible to use the Perfective with habitual meaning, expressing the iteration of a situation that would in itself be referred to by the Perfective, as in the example:[1] *každyj raz mne kazalos', čto kto-to otkryl* (Pfv.) *okno, i svežij veter vorvalsja* (Pfv.) *v bol'ničnuju palatu* 'each time it seemed to me as if someone (had) opened (Pfv.) the window and a fresh wind (had) rushed (Pfv.) into the hospital ward'. Habituality is here established by the adverbial *každyj raz* 'each time', so that the Perfective/Imperfective opposition need not be used in the subordinate clause to establish habituality, but can be used to distinguish the aspect that would be assigned to a single occurrence of the appropriate situation. Where there is no other overt marker of habituality, it is possible in Russian to introduce such sentences by *byvalo*, literally 'it used to be', which establishes habituality, then continuing with the aspectual values that would be appropriate to describing each individual occurrence of the iterated situation.[2]

In Bulgarian, with its more profuse set of aspectual forms, use can be made here of the difference between the two oppositions Perfective/Imperfective and Aorist/Imperfect, the latter only in the past tense.[3] One of the functions of the Perfective Imperfect is to describe a situation that is iterative, and each of whose individual occurrences would itself be referred to by the Perfective (in fact, the Perfective Aorist), e.g. *štom pukneše* (Pfv. Imperfect) *zorata, izkarvax ovcite navən* 'as soon as dawn broke, I used to drive the sheep out',[4] where the Perfective

---

[1] This example is from Rassudova (1968: 50). As Russian does not have a distinct Pluperfect, it is not clear out of context whether the English gloss should use the Simple Past or the Pluperfect here.

[2] For examples, see section 4.1.

[3] Although Old Russian had both Aorist and Imperfect, these forms are completely absent from the modern language. Of the other Slavonic languages that retain the Aorist and Imperfect, not all allow all four combinations (Perfective Aorist, Imperfective Aorist, Perfective Imperfect, Imperfective Imperfect): in Upper Sorbian, for instance, only the Perfective Aorist and the Imperfective Imperfect exist (Šewc 1968: 178), e.g. Perfective Aorist *kupi* 'he bought', Imperfective Imperfect *kupowaše* 'he was buying, used to buy', but not **kupiše*, **kupowa*.

[4] Beaulieux and Mladenov (1950: 335).

Imperfect *pukneše*, referring to the dawn breaking, both indicates that on each specific occasion I would have said, using the Perfective Aorist, *štom pukna zorata*, . . . 'as soon as dawn broke . . .', and that this was a habitual occurrence. At this point it is worth recapitulating briefly on the meaning of the Bulgarian Imperfective Aorist and Perfective Imperfect, both of which combine perfectivity and imperfectivity, but are by no means synonymous. The Imperfective Aorist takes a situation which is described by an imperfective form (Imperfective), to give explicit reference to its internal complexity, and circumscribes the situation by giving it a perfective form (Aorist), i.e. the function of the Imperfective Aorist could be described as the perfective of an imperfective, or the Aorist of the Imperfective. The Perfective Imperfect, on the other hand, takes a situation which would in itself be described by a perfective form (Perfective), and then superimposes upon this imperfectivity, or rather one of the possible subtypes of imperfectivity, namely habituality, i.e. this is the imperfective (or, more specifically, the habitual) of a perfective, or the Imperfect of the Perfective. In other words, the difference between the Imperfective Aorist and the Perfective Imperfect derives from the different hierarchical ordering of the features of perfectivity and imperfectivity: in the former perfectivity dominates imperfectivity, in the latter imperfectivity dominates perfectivity.

In Georgian, too, where the Perfective/Imperfective and Aorist/ Imperfect oppositions are formally distinct in the past tense, the Perfective Imperfect can be used to describe a habitual situation each of whose occurrences would in itself be described by a purely perfective form (Perfective Aorist), e.g. *i ḳacebma meṭad daigvianes! çamoiȝaxoda xolme xširad salome, gamovidoda, miidebda šublʒe xels da gaixedavda gzaze* 'those men are verily late! Salome used often to cry, go outside, put her hands to her eyes, and look towards the road', where each of *çamoiȝaxoda, gamovidoda, miidebda,* and *gaixedavda* is Perfective Imperfect.[1]

1.2.2. *Progressive*

In the present section we shall consider the meaning of specifically progressive forms, such as English *John is singing*, Spanish *Juan está cantando*, Italian *Gianni sta cantando*, Icelandic *Jón er að syngja*, Irish *tá Seán ag canadh*. Although most of the illustrative examples will be taken from English, it should be noted from the outset

---

[1] Vogt (1971: 189–90).

that the English Progressive has, in comparison with progressive forms in many other languages, an unusually wide range. Some of the uses of the English Progressive that are not shared by progressive forms in other languages will be noted towards the end of this section. In some languages, the distinction between progressive and nonprogressive meaning by means of progressive and nonprogressive forms is obligatory, whereas in others the use of the specifically progressive forms is optional, i.e. the nonprogressive form does not exclude progressive meaning. English belongs to the first type, so that Progressive and non-Progressive are not in general interchangeable, nor can any one of these in general be replaced by the other; in Spanish and Italian, on the other hand, it is normally possible to replace the Progressive by other forms, without implying nonprogressive meaning, so that corresponding to English *John is singing* Spanish may have either *Juan está cantando* (Progressive) or *Juan canta*; similarly Italian may have either *Gianni sta cantando* or *Gianni canta*. French has a specifically progressive form, *Jean est en train de chanter*, but it is even less frequently used than the Spanish or Italian Progressives, so that *John is singing* will normally be translated into French as *Jean chante*.

Definitions of progressiveness found in some traditional grammars, along the lines of describing a situation in progress, often fail to bring out the difference between progressiveness and imperfectivity. For this reason, one of the main tasks of the present section will be to explain progressiveness in terms of how it differs from imperfectivity as a whole. Firstly, imperfectivity includes as a special case habituality, and a situation can be viewed as habitual without its being viewed as progressive, as with the English non-Progressive Habitual in *John used to write poems* (contrasting with the Progressive *John used to be writing poems*). In this respect, progressiveness is similar to continuousness, which is definable as imperfectivity that is not occasioned by habituality. As examples like *John used to be writing poems* show, progressiveness is not incompatible with habituality: a given situation can be viewed both as habitual, and as progressive, i.e. each individual occurrence of the situation is presented as being progressive, and the sum total of all these occurrences is presented as being habitual (the habitual of a progressive). However, habituality on its own is not sufficient to require or allow the use of specifically progressive forms. In a language where progressive and nonprogressive forms are not distinguished, or are not distinguished obligatorily, such as French, then the nonprogressive

33

imperfective forms will clearly have wider range than does the English non-Progressive. Thus, in French *chaque jour à cinq heures le poète écrivait un poème* may have the specifically imperfective Imperfect *écrivait* here simply by virtue of habituality (i.e. 'each day at five o'clock the poet wrote a poem'), or by virtue of the fact that the poem-writing situation was ongoing at five o'clock each day (i.e. 'each day at five o'clock the poet was writing a poem'). Other languages with distinct progressive forms are like English in this respect, as in Brazilian Portuguese *todas as tardes, quando ele chegava* (Imperfect) *em casa, as crianças estavam brincando* (Progressive) *na rua* 'every evening, when he returned (Imperfect) home, the children were playing (Progressive) in the street'.[1] Just as habituality does not determine progressiveness, so equally progressiveness does not determine habituality, i.e. a situation can be viewed as progressive without being viewed as habitual, as in *John was writing a poem at five o'clock on the fifth of June 1975 A.D.* (not **John used to write/used to be writing a poem at five o'clock on the fifth of June 1975 A.D.*, since the specification of the one occasion on which the situation took place excludes the possibility of habitual meaning). One might still conclude, however, that progressiveness is the same as continuousness, since continuousness is itself imperfectivity not determined by habituality.

If we continue comparing languages with special progressive forms and those without, then we find that even if we exclude sentences with habitual meaning, the range of progressiveness is still narrower than that of nonprogressive forms. Thus if we take the French sentence *Jean savait qu'il parlait trop vite*, with two Imperfects (*savait*, from *savoir* 'to know', and *parlait*, from *parler* 'speak'), and assume a nonhabitual interpretation, then it is possible for the second verb to appear in the Progressive in English (indeed necessary that it should do so, in this interpretation of the French sentence), but impossible for the first verb to appear in the Progressive: *John knew/*was knowing that he was speaking too quickly*. If we look at other languages with specifically progressive forms, then the same situation holds, for instance in Spanish (with the proviso that Spanish does not require overt specification of progressive meaning, so that the nonprogressive form is also possible in the second clause): *Juan sabía* (Imperfect)/**estaba sabiendo* (Progressive) *que hablaba* (Imperfect)/*estaba hablando* (Progressive) *demasiado de prisa*. Taking further examples of this kind, we find that

---

[1] Thomas (1969: 202).

verbs tend to divide into two disjoint (nonoverlapping) classes, those that can appear in the progressive forms, and those that cannot. Moreover, this distinction corresponds[1] to that between stative and nonstative verbs. Thus we can give the general definition of progressiveness as the combination of progressive meaning and nonstative meaning. Naturally, then, stative verbs do not have progressive forms, since this would involve an internal contradiction between the stativity of the verb and the nonstativity essential to the progressive.

Given this characterisation of the progressive, one might expect different languages with progressive forms to agree on when these progressive forms can be used. Unfortunately, this is not the situation that we actually observe, since different languages in fact have different rules for determining when explicitly progressive forms can be used. In English and Spanish, for instance, the explicitly progressive form can be used in the sentences *it is raining, está lluviendo*. In Icelandic, on the other hand, only the nonprogressive form is possible here: *hann/það rignir* (not **hann/það er að rigna*).[2] In English, it is not in general possible to use progressive forms of verbs of inert perception like *see*, *hear* (though some exceptions will be noted below), i.e. not **I am seeing you there under the table*, or **you aren't hearing*. In Portuguese, however, such forms are perfectly acceptable: *estou te vendo lá embaixo da mesa; você não está ouvindo*.[3] In these particular cases, the relevant factor seems to be that it is possible to view raining, seeing, hearing, etc., either as states or as non-states (dynamic situations): different psychological theories differ as to just how active a process perception is, and there is no reason to suppose that language presupposes the answer by uniquely classifying perception as either a state or a dynamic situation. Different languages are free to choose, essentially as an arbitrary choice, whether such verbs are classified as stative or not.[4]

---

[1] More so in the other languages than in English, where many stative verbs also appear in the Progressive; see further below.

[2] Einarsson (1949: 144).

[3] Thomas (1969: 200–1).

[4] This does not of course imply any necessary difference in cognition between languages with stative verbs here and those with nonstative verbs. The explanation at this point may seem completely circular: progressiveness is defined in terms of stativity, but is then taken as sufficient evidence for classifying a given verb as stative or nonstative, i.e. Portuguese *ver* 'see' can occur in the Progressive because it is non-stative, and it is nonstative because it can occur in the Progressive. However, the argument depends on there being a sufficiently large class

So far, we have tacitly assumed that some verbs are stative, others not, i.e. that this is a matter of classification of lexical items into disjoint (nonoverlapping) sets. In English, however, this is not the case: there are many verbs that are treated sometimes as stative, sometimes as nonstative, depending on the particular meaning they have in the given sentence. One such verb is the English verb *be*, so that in addition to *Fred is silly* we have *Fred is being silly*. The second of these can be paraphrased by *Fred is acting in a silly manner*, with the nonstative verb *act*, whereas this is not possible in the first case. The first sentence does not imply that Fred is doing anything silly at the moment, indeed he may be behaving quite sensibly at the moment, the only claim is that in general he is silly; the second refers specifically to the way Fred is behaving at the moment, and makes no claim beyond this about his behaviour at other times. Other languages have a more strict lexical classification here: in Italian, for instance, *essere* 'be' is stative, and there is no Progressive for this verb, i.e. no **sto essendo* 'I am being'. Even in English, lexical as opposed to semantic classification is to some extent involved, so that one finds synonymous or nearly synonymous constructions where in the one case the Progressive is possible, and in the other not, e.g. *he is suffering from influenza* and *he is (*is being) ill with influenza*:[1] in general *suffer* is a nonstative verb, and the Progressive is possible even when it is being used as synonymous with a stative verb. In English, the general rule seems to be that lexically stative verbs can be used nonstatively and appear in the Progressive, while lexically nonstative verbs do not lose their ability to be in the Progressive by being used statively.

Another nonstative use of stative verbs in English is in sentences like *I'm understanding more about quantum mechanics as each day goes by*. Normally, the verb *understand* is stative, so that if someone asks whether what he is saying is comprehensible, it is possible to answer *yes, I understand you*, but not **yes, I'm understanding you*. In the example given above with the Progressive of *understand*, however, the reference is not to an unchanging state of comprehension, the degree of comprehension being the same from one time-point to another, but rather of a change in the degree of understanding: on any given day, I understood

of clear cases where different languages do agree on the assignment of stativity. If the argument led to our classifying the translation equivalents of *die, kill,* and *hit* in some language as stative, then this would strongly suggest that the argument was wrong.

[1] This example from Leech (1971: 20).

more about quantum mechanics than on any previous day. Thus the verb *understand* here refers not to a state, but to a developing process, whose individual phases are essentially different from one another.

Even if we allow for nonstative uses of basically stative verbs, however, there are still some uses of the English Progressive that are not accounted for. Thus such verbs as *live, stand* (in the sense of being in a certain position, rather than of assuming that position) are stative, and in most languages with distinct progressive forms may not appear in the progressive, while in English their progressive forms are used, and contrast with the corresponding nonprogressive forms, as in *I live at 6 Railway Cuttings* and *I'm living at 6 Railway Cuttings*, or *the Sphinx stands by the Nile* and *Mr. Smith is standing by the Nile*. In such pairs, the non-Progressive refers to a more or less permanent state of affairs, whereas the Progressive refers to a more temporary state. Thus if I say *I live at 6 Railway Cuttings*, I imply that this is my normal residence, whereas if I say *I'm living at 6 Railway Cuttings*, I imply that this is only a temporary residence (for instance, while my Mayfair flat is being redecorated). Similarly in the examples with *stand*: the Sphinx is a reasonably permanent fixture on the banks of the Nile, while we might expect Mr. Smith to be a temporary feature, standing there for a very limited period of time. Equally, the English Progressive can refer to a habitual situation that holds for a relatively limited period, as in *we're going to the opera a lot these days, at that time I was working the night shift*.

In addition to this use of the Progressive in English, the Progressive in English has a number of other specific uses that do not seem to fit under the general definition of progressiveness, for instance in *I've only had six whiskies and already I'm seeing pink elephants* (Progressive of the stative verb *see*, in the sense that I am only imagining things, in fact there are no pink elephants for me to see), or *she's always buying far more vegetables than they can possibly eat* (where the function of the Progressive seems simply to be to add greater emotive effect than would be achieved by the straightforward *she always buys far more vegetables than they can possibly eat*).[1] Finally, some uses seem to be purely

---

[1] Einarsson (1949: 144–5) notes that in Icelandic many verbs that normally do not occur in the Progressive can occur in the Progressive for emotive effect, e.g. *til hvers ertu að búa á Ási?*, literally 'why are you living at Ás? with the sense of 'why on earth do you live at Ás?' (surprise or disgust). J. Lyons suggests to me that the dynamic nature of the progressive may well account for its use to denote situations that are unexpected (i.e. not as they should be, cp. the use of the Progressive in English for temporary

idiosyncratic: thus while one can say either *you look well* or *you're looking well*, with *seem*, as opposed to *look*, the Progressive is impossible, i.e. only *you seem well*, not **you're seeming well*; similarly with *sound* in the appropriate sense: *you sound hoarse*, not **you're sounding hoarse*.

These examples demonstrate that in English the meaning of the Progressive has extended well beyond the original definition of progressivity as the combination of continuous meaning and nonstativity. The question then arises whether the English Progressive should be given some other definition than the general linguistic definition of progressiveness, i.e. whether the meaning of the English Progressive is so extended that we should not speak of a basic progressive meaning with various subsidiary meanings, but rather of some more general basic meaning which includes both progressive meaning and the various other meanings that the English Progressive has. For instance, one might suggest that the basic meaning of the English Progressive is to indicate a contingent situation: this would subsume progressive meaning itself, and also the use of the Progressive to indicate a temporary (contingent) state, and its use to indicate a contingent habitual situation. This may well be the direction in which the English Progressive is developing diachronically, but does not give a completely adequate characterisation of its function in the modern language. As noted in the above discussion, there are several idiosyncrasies in the use of the English Progressive that seem, at least in the present state of research, to militate against a general meaning being able to account for every single use of this form. Moreover, although many stative verbs can be used in the Progressive to indicate a contingent state, it is by no means the case that all stative verbs can be used in this way.[1] For instance, the verb *know* does not allow formation of a Progressive, even with reference to a contingent state (*John realised that there was no sugar before Mary came in, and forgot that there was no sugar almost as soon as she went out, so that when Mary was in the room he knew/*was knowing that there was no sugar*),

states, or surprise), or indeed given as unreal (as with seeing pink elephants). While this suggestion is speculative, it may go some way towards providing an explanation for the apparently multifarious meanings that the English Progressive has. See further footnote 1, page 49.

[1] For a classification of verbs into those that may occur in the Progressive and those that may not, see Leech (1971: 14–27); the same framework is used in the briefer discussion of the Progressive in Quirk et al. (1972: 92–7).

even with reference to a surprising state (*fancy that! you know/*are knowing all about quantum mechanics*), even with reference to a counter-factual state (*so you know/*are knowing all about quantum mechanics, do/ are you?*), even with reference to a changing degree of knowledge (*I find that I know/*am knowing more about quantum mechanics with each day that passes*). Thus the extension of the English Progressive is more restricted than that of contingent state, although, as suggested above, it may well be that English is developing from a restricted use of the Progressive, always with progressive meaning, to this more extended meaning range, the present anomalies representing a midway stage between these two points.[1]

The diachronic development may be compared with that in the Celtic languages. In the present tense, Irish has distinct Progressive and non-Progressive, i.e. the Progressive *tá sé ag dul* 'he is going' has specifically progressive meaning. In Welsh, the form with the same etymological origin as the Irish Progressive has extended its range to cover nonprogressive habitual meaning and stative meaning, as in *y mae ef yn mynd* 'he is going' or 'he goes', *y mae ef yn hoffi coffi* 'he likes coffee'; the Simple Present remains only for a small number of stative verbs. In Scots Gaelic, this originally progressive form is now the only present for nearly all verbs, barring a few exceptions like the verb 'be', so that *tha e a' dol* means either 'he is going' or 'he goes'.

Although the *-ing* form is an essential ingredient of the English Progressive, in nonfinite constructions without the auxiliary *be* the *-ing* form does not necessarily have progressive meaning; in fact, in such constructions it typically indicates only simultaneity (relative present time reference) with the situation of the main verb, as: *knowing that Bill was on holiday, I burgled his house* (i.e. *as I knew*, not **as I was knowing*); *anyone knowing the whereabouts of John Smith is asked to communicate with his solicitor* (i.e. *anyone who knows*, not **anyone who is knowing*); *Fred('s) knowing the answer to the problem of life and death amazed the theology professor* (i.e. *the fact that Fred knew*, not **the fact that Fred was knowing*). Where the sense is progressive in such constructions, there is no overt indicator of progressive meaning in English, as in *walking down the street, I met an old friend* (not **being walking*, despite *while I was walking*); *the man walking down the street now is a*

---

[1] Cp. the suggestion by Schopf (1974a: 26) that affective (emotive) uses of the Progressive in English indicate the start of the breakdown of the current system.

sociologist (not **the man being walking down the street now*, despite *the man who is walking down the street now*).[1]

There is, however, one nonfinite construction where the *-ing* form does have specifically progressive force, namely after verbs of perception. Thus the difference between *I saw the accused stab the victim* and *I saw the accused stabbing the victim* is one of aspect: *stab* is non-Progressive (in fact, it has perfective meaning, since the sense is that I witnessed the whole of the act of stabbing, and am not dividing the act up into separate beginning, middle and end, but presenting it as a single complete whole); *stabbing* is Progressive (it is not necessary for me to have witnessed the beginning and/or end of the process, but only the middle, at least this is all I am alluding to). Similarly: *I watched Fred sit for a whole hour doing nothing*, where Fred's sitting, no matter how long it lasted, is presented as a single complete situation, in contrast to *I watched Fred sitting doing nothing*.

---

[1] Seuren (1974: 4) notes that some derived nominals have an overt aspectual distinction, e.g. *thieving* (imperfective meaning) versus *theft* (perfective meaning), cp. also the plural *thefts*. While there is indeed aspectual differentiation in some such pairs, the distinction is not that between progressive and nonprogressive meaning.

2

Aspect and inherent meaning

2.0.   In chapter 1, we considered oppositions between perfective and imperfective forms, and between habitual and continuous forms, largely irrespective of the particular lexical items exhibiting the contrasts. The main exceptions to this generalisation are the discussion in section 1.1.2 of combinations of perfectivity with lexical or other specification of the internal structure of a situation, and the discussion of the progressive in section 1.2.2 where it was noted that progressiveness is intimately bound up with the inherent nonstativity of the situation being described. In the present chapter we shall look in somewhat more detail at inherent aspectual (i.e. semantic aspectual) properties of various classes of lexical items, and see how these interact with other aspectual oppositions, either prohibiting certain combinations, or severely restricting their meaning.

2.1.   Punctual and durative[1]

In section 1.1.2, we noted that it is quite possible to have perfective forms of verbs describing situations that must inherently last for a certain period of time, as in Russian *ja postojal* (Pfv.) *tam čas* 'I stood there for an hour'. We may therefore make a distinction between imperfectivity and durativity, where imperfectivity means viewing a situation with regard to its internal structure (duration, phasal sequences), and durativity simply refers to the fact that the given situation lasts for a certain period of time (or at least, is conceived of as lasting for a certain period of time); the verb *postojal* in the example quoted above is thus durative, although not imperfective. The opposite of durativity

---

[1] In some terminological systems, the terms 'punctual' and 'durative' are used in essentially the same sense as our terms 'perfective' and 'continuous', respectively. In the present work, the two sets of terms are not equivalent, as will become apparent in the discussion below.

is punctuality, which thus means the quality of a situation that does not last in time (is not conceived of as lasting in time), one that takes place momentarily. It should be noted that the crucial point here is that punctual situations do not have any duration, not even duration of a very short period. Thus a punctual situation, by definition, has no internal structure, and in a language with separate imperfective forms to indicate reference to the internal structure of a situation, then clearly punctuality and imperfectivity will be incompatible.

So far, we have rather taken for granted that there are punctual situations, but we must now investigate in further detail the precise range of possibilities in this area. One verb which is often quoted as an example of a punctual verb is the English verb *cough*, and its translation equivalents in other languages, referring to a single cough, rather than a series of coughs.[1] If this were strictly true, then the Progressive, which has imperfective meaning, would be impossible with *cough* (on the interpretation when there is only one cough), i.e. *he was coughing* would be inappropriate in referring to a situation where he gave a single cough; the same would be true of French *il toussait* (Imperfect), for instance. The only interpretation possible for such a sentence would be that the reference is to a series of coughs, since a series of coughs, even if there are only two coughs, is clearly a durative situation. At this stage, we may introduce the terms 'semelfactive' to refer to a situation that takes place once and once only (e.g. one single cough),[2] and 'iterative' to refer to a situation that is repeated (e.g. a series of coughs). Thus the inherent punctuality of *cough* would restrict the range of interpretations that can be given to imperfective forms of this verb.

Objections have been raised to this analysis of verbs like *cough*, on the grounds that in fact the single act of coughing, for instance, is not punctual in the strict sense, but rather refers to a situation that lasts for a very short time. For as long as we are in real time, it is unlikely that anyone would want to refer to the duration or successive phases that make up this situation, but this restriction can be lifted by, for instance,

---

[1] Strictly speaking, it is the situation, rather than the verb, that is punctual, though for convenience we shall retain the traditional practice of using the term 'punctual verb' for a verb referring to a punctual situation.

[2] This is in accordance with the etymology of the term (Latin *semel* 'once'), but differs somewhat from its use in, for instance, Slavonic linguistics, where the verb *kašljanut'* 'cough' is described as semelfactive, even when it is used in a sentence like *on kašljanul pjat' raz* 'he coughed five times', where the situation is clearly iterative.

imagining a situation where someone is commenting on a slowed down film which incorporates someone's single cough, as for instance in an anatomy lecture: here, it would be quite appropriate for the lecturer to comment on the relevant part of the film *and now the subject is coughing*, even in referring to a single cough, since the single act of coughing has now been extended, and is clearly durative, in that the relevant film sequence lasts for a certain period of time. The question would then arise as to whether there are any kinds of situation which, even if slowed down, would have to be strictly punctual. Clearly coughing would not enter this category, and it is in fact difficult to think of clear examples that would. One possible example would be a situation of the sort described in the sentence *John reached the summit of the mountain*: here there is one moment when John had not yet reached the summit, and another moment when he had, with no time intervening between the two. No matter how slowly one presented the film of John's mountaineering exploits, the interval between these two moments would always be zero, and it would always be inappropriate to say *at this point, John is reaching the summit*. Imperfective forms of *reach the summit* would then only have iterative meaning, as in *the soldiers are already reaching the summit* (i.e. some have already reached it, some have not yet reached it, there being several individual acts of reaching the summit).[1]

But even with verbs like *cough*, we find that some languages do have a special class of verbs, formally marked, which refer to situations that under normal circumstances cannot be viewed as having any duration, in the absence of iterativity.[2] In Russian, for instance, there is a large class of verbs with the suffix *-nu*, all Perfective, without strict aspectual partners in the Imperfective Aspect, such as *kašljanut'* 'cough', *blesnut'* 'flash'.[3] In Hungarian, too, there are several suffixes which serve in general to mark verbs of this class, such as *zörren* 'knock, give a knock' (cf. *zörög* 'knock' (possibly repeatedly)).[4] Thus a number of languages

---

[1] Compare the discussion in Vendler (1967) of what are there referred to by the term 'achievements'.

[2] In Slavonic linguistics, the term 'semelfactive' (Russian *odnokratnyj*) or 'momentary' (Russian *mgnovennyj*) is given to such verbs, qua lexical items, irrespective of whether they are used iteratively or not.

[3] Isačenko (1962: 398–402); there are often derivationally related Imperfective verbs, with the same lexical meaning except insofar as they are not punctual, e.g. *kašljat'*, *blestet'*.

[4] Majtinskaja (1959: 117–19).

do recognise a class of verbs that under normal circumstances can only refer to punctual situations (or iteration of punctual acts), suggesting that punctuality is a valid linguistic category, notwithstanding the apparent difficulties caused by recent technology (in particular, slowing down of films) in distinguishing the precise range of punctual situations.

2.2. Telic and atelic[1]

We may start the discussion of this section by contrasting some of the semantic aspectual properties of the situations described by the two sentences *John is singing* and *John is making a chair*. Both refer to durative situations, since both singing and making a chair are situations that can, indeed must, be conceived of as lasting a certain amount of time; moreover, it is possible for both of these situations to last for a short or for a long time, depending, for instance, on John's stamina when it comes to singing, and the speed with which he makes chairs. However, there is an important difference between these two types of situations with regard to their internal structure. In the second example, there comes eventually a point at which John completes the action of making a chair, the chair is ready, and at this point the situation described by *make a chair* must of necessity come to an end; moreover, until this point is reached, the situation described by *make a chair* cannot come to an end, but can only be broken off part way through. This is not true of the situation described by *John is singing*: John can stop singing at any point, and it will still be true that he has sung, even if he has not completed the song or songs he set out to sing. Thus the situation described by *make a chair* has built into it a terminal point, namely that point at which the chair is complete, when it automatically terminates; the situation described by *sing* has no such terminal point, and can be protracted indefinitely or broken off at any point. Situations like that described by *make a chair* are called telic, those like that described by *sing* atelic. The telic nature of a situation can often be tested in the following way: if a sentence referring to this situation in a form with imperfective meaning (such as the English Progressive) implies the sentence referring to the same situation in a form with perfect meaning (such as the English Perfect), then the situation is atelic; otherwise it is telic. Thus from *John is singing* one can deduce *John has sung*, but from

[1] The term 'telic situation' corresponds to the term 'accomplishment' used, for instance, by Vendler (1967: 102). The term 'telic' was apparently introduced by Garey (1957) (cp. Ancient Greek *télos* 'end').

John is making a chair one cannot deduce *John has made a chair*.[1] Thus a telic situation is one that involves a process that leads up to a well-defined terminal point, beyond which the process cannot continue.

In the preceding paragraph, we spoke of telic situations, rather than telic verbs. At first sight, it might seem that we could call verbs that refer to telic situations telic, those that refer to atelic situations atelic; in fact, the picture is not quite so simple. If it were, then we could, for instance, call *drown* a telic verb (drowning is a process that necessarily comes to an end when the animal drowning dies), and *sing* an atelic verb. However, situations are not described by verbs alone, but rather by the verb together with its arguments (subject and objects).[2] Thus although *John is singing* describes an atelic situation, the sentence *John is singing a song* describes a telic situation, since this situation has a well-defined terminal point, namely when John comes to the end of the song in question. *John is singing songs* is again atelic, whereas *John is singing five songs* is again telic.[3] Similarly, although *John is drowning* describes a telic situation, the sentence *cats drown if you put them in deep water* is not telic, since it refers to an ongoing tendency for cats to drown, a tendency that can go on indefinitely, irrespective of the number of cats who have completed their act of drowning. Moreover, provided an appropriate context is provided, many sentences that would otherwise

---

[1] Compare the discussion in Klein (1974: 106–7), with the examples: *Si quelqu'un jouait, et tout en jouant a été interrompu, est-ce qu'il a joué? Oui, il a joué* 'If someone was playing, and while playing was interrupted, has he played? Yes, he has played' (atelic), versus: *Si quelqu'un se noyait, et tout en se noyant a été interrompu, est-ce qu'il s'est noyé? Non, il ne s'est pas noyé* 'If someone was drowning, and while drowning was interrupted, has he drowned? No, he hasn't drowned' (telic).

[2] See, for further discussion, Dowty (1972), Verkuyl (1972). Some of the sentences that give difficulty to Vendler (1967: 104) in his discussion of related problems seem to stem from the failure to realise that subjects, as well as objects, must be included here. More generally, although aspect, and tense and mood, are usually indicated in the verbal morphology, they do not so much characterise the verb itself as the whole of the sentence, including subjects and objects.

[3] Actually, it is difficult to think of sentences which must be interpreted as describing a telic situation. Thus if John were to repeat the same song incessantly, then even *John is singing a song* would be atelic. The sentence *John is killing Mary* might seem to describe a necessary telic situation, which must come to an end when Mary is dead, but even this is so only given our knowledge about the real world, where dead people do not come to life again, thus forestalling the possibility that they might be killed iteratively. One could easily imagine an advance in surgery that would make an atelic interpretation of *John is killing Mary* perfectly reasonable.

be taken to describe atelic situations can be given a telic interpretation. Imagine, for instance, a singing class where each of the pupils is required to sing a certain set passage; then the verb *sing* on its own, in this context, may be taken to mean 'sing the set passage', so that from *John is singing* it will not follow that *John has sung.* Similarly, in a classroom situation where the pupils are taking turns at reading, *John has read* will have the specific interpretation that he has completed his turn.[1] However, although it is difficult to find sentences that are unambiguously telic or atelic, this does not affect the general semantic distinction made between telic and atelic situations.

The particular importance of the telic/atelic distinction for the study of aspect is that, when combined with the perfective/imperfective opposition, the semantic range of telic verbs is restricted considerably, so that certain logical deductions can be made from the aspect of a sentence referring to a telic situation that cannot be made from the aspect of a sentence referring to an atelic situation. For instance, a perfective form referring to a telic situation implies attainment of the terminal point of that situation,[2] as in Russian *on sdelal* (Pfv.) *stul,* French *il fit* (Past Definite)/*a fait* (Perfect) *une chaise* 'he made/has made a chair', both of which imply that the chair was completed. The imperfective forms carry no such implication, and imply rather that the chair had not been completed at the time referred to: *il faisait* (Imperfect) *une chaise, he was making* (Progressive) *a chair.*[3]

In some languages, it is possible to derive verbs referring to specifically telic situations from verbs that do not necessarily refer to telic situations, usually as part of the derivational morphology. In German, for instance, there is a contrast between *kämpfen* 'fight' (possibly without achieving anything) and *erkämpfen* 'achieve by means of a fight', the latter referring to a process of fighting that leads up to some terminal point. A similar difference exists between *essen* and the specifically telic *aufessen,* and between the English glosses thereto: *eat* and *eat up.* In Latin, the same relation obtains between *facere* 'make, do' and its

[1] Thus Dowty (1972: 28) comments: 'I have not been able to find a single activity verb which cannot have an accomplishment [i.e. telic – B.C.] sense in at least some special context'.

[2] Such examples may have given rise to the widespread view that perfectivity indicates completedness.

[3] In Russian, the Imperfective can also be occasioned by the unmarked nature of the Imperfective, rather than by specifically imperfective meaning; see chapter 6. Thus, strictly, no implication as to the completion or noncompletion of the chair can be drawn from *on delal stul.*

derivative *conficere* 'complete'.[1] Thus the German sentence *die Partisanen haben für die Freiheit ihres Landes gekämpft* 'the partisans have
fought for the freedom of their country' does not imply that their fight
was successful, whereas *die Partisanen haben die Freiheit ihres Landes
erkämpft* does.

In expressions referring to telic situations it is important that there
should be both a process leading up to the terminal point as well as the
terminal point. Thus the example quoted above, *John reached the
summit*, is not telic, since one cannot speak of the process leading up to
John's reaching the summit by saying *John is reaching the summit*.[2]
In general, it is easy to distinguish telic situations from those Vendler
calls achievements, though there are some difficult cases. With a telic
situation, it is possible to use a verbal form with imperfective meaning,
the implication being that at the time in question the terminal point
had not yet been reached; indeed, it is possible to state explicitly that the
terminal point was never reached, as in *Mary was singing a song when
she died*. Achievements preclude the use of specifically imperfective
forms, so that we do not have **John was reaching the summit when he
died*, but only, for instance, *John had almost reached the summit when he
died*. A more difficult case is the English verb *die*.[3] Although this refers
to a punctual situation, yet it is still possible to say *John is dying*, which
refers to the process leading up to John's death, and might therefore
seem to make *die* a telic verb. However, it seems odd to say *?John was
dying, but the discovery of a new medicine led to his recovery*. In other
words, although *John was dying* implies that at the time in question he
was not yet dead, yet still it seems to imply that he did die (later);
similarly, *John is dying* holds out little if any hope for his recovery,
unlike *Mary is singing a song*, where it is still possible that she will be
prevented from completing the song. This suggests that a new class
of situations will have to be recognised, referring to a punctual event
and the immediately preceding process, in the sense that the process

---

[1] Strictly, these verbs involve predications, rather than situations, which
are telic, since the addition of an indefinitely plural subject, for instance,
means that the whole situation is not telic, as in *some children eat their
food up*; cp. the example *cats drown* . . . above.

[2] Vendler (1967: 102–3) uses the term 'achievement' for situations like
John reached the summit: the reference is to the end-point of a process
only, which is why, as we noted in section 2.1, such situations are punctual
in the strictest sense of the term.

[3] Vendler (1967: 107) assigns *die* without reservation to the class of
achievements.

47

preceding the event is so intimately bound up with the event that once the process is under way the event cannot be prevented from occurring. It is interesting that Russian differs from English here, since in Russian it is quite possible to say *Kolja umiral* (Ipfv.), *no ne umer* (Pfv.) 'Kolya was dying, but didn't die'; in other words *umirat'/umeret'* 'die' in Russian is telic, referring to the process leading up to death, whether or not death is reached. Similarly, Russian *on ugovarival* (Ipfv.) *menja, no ne ugovoril* (Pfv.) does not really translate into good English as 'he was persuading me, but didn't persuade me'; Russian *ugovarivat'/ugovorit'* 'persuade' is telic, whereas English *persuade* can only refer to the process leading up to the moment of persuasion if that process is in fact successful.

2.3. State and dynamic situation

The distinction between states and dynamic situations[1] is one that seems reasonably clear intuitively, and in practice one finds a large measure of agreement between individuals who are asked to classify situations as static or dynamic, and similarly between languages that have overt correlates of the static/dynamic distinction, although there are some instances of disagreement, as was noted in section 1.2.2 on the progressive. The present section will attempt to clarify the distinction between states and dynamic situations, and also the meaning of certain related terms, such as 'event' and 'process'.[2]

We may approach the problem by considering a situation that is extended in time, i.e. restricting ourselves initially to durative situations. The term 'phase' will be used to refer to a situation at any given point of time in its duration.[3] As examples to work with, we may consider first of all the verb *know*, referring to a state, and the verb *run*, referring to a dynamic situation. One difference between the situations referred

---

[1] In other discussions of this distinction, the opposition is often made using the terms 'state' and 'action'. Some linguists, however, use the term 'action' in a more restricted sense, for a dynamic situation that requires the involvement of an agent; thus *the stone is rolling down the hill* would not be an action in this narrower sense of the term. To avoid possible confusion, the more explicit term 'dynamic situation' is used here.

[2] For further discussion, see Lyons (1963: 111–19), Lakoff (1966), Vendler (1967: 107–21).

[3] This is a slight extension of the dictionary definition of 'phase', which usually restricts the term to a changing or developing process at different points of time.

to by these two verbs is in the relation between different phases of the situation: in the case of *know*, all phases of the situation *John knows where I live* are identical; whichever point of time we choose to cut in on the situation of John's knowledge, we shall find exactly the same situation. With *run*, however, this is not so: if we say *John is running*, then different phases of the situation will be very different: at one moment John will have one foot on the ground, at another moment neither foot will be on the ground, and so on. Thus *know*, on the one hand, involves no change, whereas *run* involves necessarily change. This gives a first approximation of the characterisation of state versus dynamic situation.

However, there are still some states and non-states which this dichotomy does not correctly characterise. The state of standing (i.e. being in a standing position) may involve no change, but equally it does not exclude the possibility of change: thus I can say of one of my books that it stands on such-and-such a shelf even if its position on the shelf changes (e.g. if I move it every now and again). One might therefore suggest that dynamic situations involve necessarily change, whereas states are situations that may or may not involve change. But there are still difficult cases. In the situation referred to by the sentence *the oscilloscope is emitting a pure tone at 300 cycles per second*, we have a dynamic situation that does not involve any necessary change, at least not any change that would be apparent to someone unacquainted with the operation of the oscilloscope, although this would not affect his conception of the dynamic nature of the situation. These exceptional cases can in fact be brought under a slightly modified characterisation of the difference between states and dynamic situations. With a state, unless something happens to change that state, then the state will continue: this applies equally to standing and to knowing. With a dynamic situation, on the other hand, the situation will only continue if it is continually subject to a new input of energy: this applies equally to running and to emitting a pure tone, since if John stops putting any effort into running, he will come to a stop, and if the oscilloscope is cut off from its source of power it will no longer emit sound. To remain in a state requires no effort, whereas to remain in a dynamic situation does require effort, whether from inside (in which case we have an agentive interpretation, e.g. *John is running*), or from outside (in which case we have a nonagentive interpretation, e.g. the oscilloscope is emitting a pure tone).[1]

[1] Developing further the speculative suggestion of footnote 1, page 37 we might further hypothesise that the use of the Progressive in English,

Since punctual situations automatically involve a change of state, they are automatically dynamic: there can be no such thing as a punctual state.

We now have a definition of state versus dynamic situation which is independent of any language-particular distinction, although we would expect language-particular distinctions that relate to this distinction (such as progressiveness as a correlate of the state/dynamic situation distinction) to dichotomise situations in more or less the same way from one language to another, with the exception of situations that can be viewed, intuitively, as either states or dynamic situations, i.e. where there might be disagreement or doubt as to whether or not the situation in question will stop unless continuously renewed.

So far, we have been referring to states as something ongoing, i.e. looking at states from within. Of course, states can also start, and cease. The start or end of a state is dynamic, since for a state to be started or stopped something must come about to bring about the change into or out of this state; this follows from the definition of state given above. Thus when, in section 1.1, we noted that states can be referred to by forms with perfective meaning, then the form describing the state here refers not only to the state, but also to its inception and termination. Thus Russian *ja postojal* (Pfv.) *tam čas* 'I stood there for an hour', Ancient Greek *ebasíleuse* (Aorist) *déka étē* 'he reigned for ten years' refer not only to the state obtaining at a given time, but also to its inception and termination, i.e. do include a dynamic element. In many languages stative verbs do not have forms with perfective meaning,[1] while in many other languages this applies to a large number of stative verbs.[2] Thus the combination of perfectivity and stativity can only have a rather restricted semantic range – reference to a state with its

typically restricted to dynamic situations, to describe contingent and make-believe states derives from a metaphorical extension of the requirement inherent in dynamic situations that they be subject to a continuing input of energy: since a contingent state is a state that is not the normal state of things, it is more difficult to maintain than an absolute state, which is the normal state of things, and to which things would be expected to revert, other things being equal. Similarly, a habitual (characteristic) situation, being a normal state of affairs, will not require the dynamic progressive form (unless the progressive is used as appropriate for each individual occurrence of a repeated series of situations making up the habitual situation), although a contingent (temporary) habitual, like a contingent state, is more likely to be in the progressive form.

[1] See, for instance, the Igbo and Yoruba examples in section 4.5.
[2] See, for instance, the Georgian examples in section 6.3.

inception and termination – and some languages do not even allow of this interpretation. Given the naturalness of the combination of stativity and imperfectivity, it is easy to see why many languages have a special form to express progressive meaning: progressive meaning combines nonstativity with continuous meaning, and in referring to non-states the distinction between continuous and perfective meaning is more important than in referring to states, which are typically continuous; thus, if a formal distinction is to be made anywhere, it is more logical for it to be made within descriptions of dynamic situations than within descriptions of static situations.

In the linguistic literature, one also comes across the terms 'event' and 'process' referring to situations. Both refer to dynamic situations; 'process' refers to the internal structure of a dynamic situation (there are thus no punctual processes), while 'event' refers to a dynamic situation as a single complete whole. Thus the term 'process' means a dynamic situation viewed imperfectively, and the term 'event' means a dynamic situation viewed perfectively.

3
Perfect

3.0. Aspect, as we have been concerned with it hitherto, has been concerned with different ways of representing the internal temporal constitution of a situation. The perfect is rather different from these aspects, since it tells us nothing directly about the situation in itself,[1] but rather relates some state to a preceding situation. As a preliminary illustration of this, to be amplified and modified in the detailed discussion below, we may contrast the English sentences *I have lost* (Perfect) *my penknife* and *I lost* (non-Perfect) *my penknife*. One possible difference between these two is that with the Perfect, there is an implication that the penknife is still lost, whereas with the non-Perfect there is no such implication. More generally, the perfect indicates the continuing present relevance of a past situation. This difference between the perfect and the other aspects has led many linguists to doubt whether the perfect should be considered an aspect at all.[2] However, given the traditional terminology in which the perfect is listed as an aspect, it seems most convenient to deal with the perfect in a book on aspect, while bearing in mind continually that it is an aspect in a rather different sense from the other aspects treated so far.

One way in which the perfect differs from the other aspects that we have examined is that it expresses a relation between two time-points, on the one hand the time of the state resulting from a prior situation, and on the other the time of that prior situation. Thus the present perfect, for instance, such as English *I have eaten*, partakes of both the present and the past. In some languages this dual role has syntactic and

---

[1] In those languages where the perfect is combinable with other aspectual categories, then these other categories may give information about the situation per se, as in the English Progressive *John has been feeding the goldfish.*

[2] A discussion of the background to this problem is given by Maslov (1962b: 30–2).

morphological repercussions. Thus in Ancient Greek, for instance, the Perfect, although referring to a past situation, is still treated as a primary (i.e. non-past) tense for the purpose of determining the sequence of tenses; even in Latin, where the so-called Perfect covers both perfect meaning and nonperfect past time reference, there is a distinction in sequence of tense, in that the Perfect with perfect meaning is usually treated as a primary tense, whereas the Perfect with nonperfect past time reference is not.[1] In some languages, the form of the perfect incorporates formal expression of the two times referred to, e.g. present and past in the present perfect; for further discussion, see section 5.2.2.0.

It should be borne in mind that the present perfect (often simply called the perfect) is only one of the possible tenses of the perfect aspect, the one that expresses a relation between present state and past situation. In other tenses we find, for instance, a past perfect (pluperfect), e.g. *John had eaten the fish*, expressing a relation between a past state and an even earlier situation; and a future perfect, e.g. *John will have eaten the fish*, expressing a relation between a future state and a situation prior to it, although there is no other specification of the absolute time of that prior action, which may be past, present, or future (e.g. *I don't know if John has eaten the fish yet, but he will have done so by the time you return*, where all that is said about the time of John's eating the fish is that it will precede some other future action, namely your returning).

In discussing the perfect, it is important not to be misled into thinking that every form that is labelled 'Perfect' in the grammar-book in fact expresses perfect meaning. Thus in Latin, for instance, as noted above, the so-called Perfect in fact covers both perfect and nonperfect meaning. The same is true of the Perfect (Compound Past) in many Romance languages, especially in their spoken forms, such as French, Italian, Romanian, though not Spanish. In some (especially southern) varieties of German the so-called Perfect has extended its sphere to take over from the Simple Past, i.e. it has in fact become the only Past Tense, quite irrespective of aspect. Most of the examples in this chapter will be from English, where there is a clear formal distinction between forms with perfect meaning, and those with nonperfect meaning.[2]

---

[1] Goodwin (1894: 91, 271); Gildersleeve and Lodge (1895: 314–19); by sequence of tenses, the tense of the verb in certain subordinate clauses is determined or restricted by the tense of the verb in the main clause.

[2] It should be noted, however, that there is some variation within English as to the precise delimitation between Perfect and non-Perfect

We may note one diagnostic characteristic of the English Perfect, which will prove useful in the ensuing discussion. This is that, in English, the Perfect may not be used together with specification of the time of the past situation, i.e. one cannot say *I have got up at five o'clock this morning*, because the specific reference to the point of time *at five o'clock this morning* is incompatible with the English Perfect. It is not specification of time as such that is excluded, since one can specify the time within which the past situation held, provided the time includes the present, e.g. *I have seen Fred today*, or even *I have seen Fred this morning* provided it is still morning at the time of speaking.[1] The experiential perfect, discussed in section 3.1.2 below, also admits of specification of a point of time, as in *I have (on some occasion in the past) got up at five o'clock*, though here *five o'clock* refers not to some specific instance of 'five o'clock', but rather ranges over all possible five o'clocks; one could not, for instance, say *I have got up at five o'clock on the sixth of June 1975 A.D.*, even as an experiential perfect. It is not clear that the mutual exclusiveness of the perfect and specification of the time of a situation is a necessary state of affairs in a language. In Spanish, for instance, where the Perfect does have specifically perfect meaning, it is still possible to specify exactly the time of the past situation, as in *me he levantado a las cinco* 'I got up at five o'clock' (in reply to a question why I am looking so tired), *Gustavo Ferrán ha muerto ayer . . . se ha estrellado anoche en los montes de nieve* 'Gustavo Ferrán died yesterday . . . he crashed last night on the snow-covered mountains', where the Perfect would be impossible in the English glosses.[2] In Russian, where there is a distinct Perfect in the passive (section 4.6), time specification is still possible with this Perfect, e.g. *dom postroen* (Perfect) *v prošlom godu* 'the house was built last year', which implies that the house is still standing, unlike *dom byl postroen* (non-Perfect) *v prošlom godu*.[3] Similarly, temporal specification is acceptable in English, provided it is

forms. In particular, American English overall shows a greater preference for the non-Perfect, in cases where British English would prefer or require the Perfect.

[1] There may be a certain amount of individual variation here: Leech (1971: 40–1) notes that some English speakers allow *I've been to the dentist this morning*, even if said in the afternoon. The Perfect in *I have recently learned that Bill is leaving* is quite generally acceptable, although *recently* here refers to some point of time in the past. See further section 3.1.4 on the recent past.

[2] Stevenson (1970: 62).

[3] Isačenko (1962: 451).

added as an afterthought to a sentence with a Perfect verb, such as *I have been to Birmingham, last week in fact,* or as a reply to a question, such as *Have you finished your article on Tibetan morphology? – Yes, last week.* At any rate, the restriction on the occurrence of temporal adverbs in English does provide a useful heuristic device for identifying the Perfect in that language.[1]

The reason why the availability of this test is so important for English is that in English, in certain nonfinite verbal constructions especially, the Perfect form (*have* plus Past Participle) does not necessarily have perfect meaning. Thus some of the following sentences with participial and infinitival constructions will be paraphrasable with finite verbs in the Perfect, others with finite verbs in the Simple Past:

> Having eaten a three-course dinner, Bill is no longer hungry (As he has eaten a three-course dinner, Bill is no longer hungry).
> Having been in Berlin before the War, Bill is surprised at the many changes (As he was in Berlin before the War, Bill is surprised at the many changes).
> Bill may already have finished his dinner (It is possible that Bill has already finished his dinner).
> Bill may have been in Berlin before the War (It is possible that Bill was in Berlin before the War).
> The judge believes Bill to have told several lies already (The judge believes that Bill has told several lies already).
> The security officer believes Bill to have been in Berlin before the War (The security officer believes that Bill was in Berlin before the War).

In such examples, even with specification of relative past time, the use of the Perfect form is possible, indeed with such nonfinite verbal forms there is no other way of indicating past time, so that in such constructions the distinction between perfect meaning and relative past time reference is not made overtly (is neutralised).

[1] The restriction against the combination of Perfect and time specification may well be part of a more general restriction against the use of the Perfect in referring to a specific occasion. The occasion may be specified by the use of an adverb of time, but it may also be presupposed by the speaker to be knowledge common to both speaker and hearer. Thus if I see you with a broken arm, then I can ask *how did you break your arm?* with the non-Perfect form, since I am taking as already given the fact that you broke your arm, and am eliciting further information about the incident. Similarly, while a past situation can be introduced into a discourse by means of the Perfect, it is thereafter common knowledge shared by speaker and hearer and will be referred to by non-Perfect forms, as in the exchange: A. *I've broken my arm.* B. *Did you break it today?*

A similar loss of overt semantic distinction emerges if we examine in more detail the English Pluperfect. A sentence like *Bill had arrived at six o'clock* is ambiguous. On the one hand, it can mean that six o'clock is the vantage point in the past from which we are observing the results of earlier events, one of which was Bill's arrival; Bill may have arrived at five o'clock, though he was still there at six. This is the strict perfect-in-the-past, i.e. denotes a past state which results from an even earlier situation; at six o'clock we would have said *Bill has arrived*. On the other hand, it is also possible to interpret the sentence in question as saying that six o'clock was the time of Bill's arrival. In this case we are simply stating that Bill's arrival preceded some other past situation (past-in-the-past), without there being any relation between Bill's arrival and any state in existence at the time of this later situation; e.g. *Bill had arrived at six o'clock and had left again at seven; the inspector did not get there until eight*. The same is true of the Future Perfect, which can be either a perfect-in-the-future, or a past-in-the-future.

3.1. Types of perfect

So far, we have given a general definition of the perfect as the continuing relevance of a previous situation. In this section, we shall examine some more specific manifestations of this general property. Not all languages that have forms with perfect meaning have the full range of the meanings listed below, while in some languages there are distinct forms for some of these meanings. The particular types of perfect discussed below are the perfect of result, the experiential perfect, the perfect of persistent situation, and the perfect of recent past.

3.1.1. *Perfect of result*

In the perfect of result, a present state is referred to as being the result of some past situation: this is one of the clearest manifestations of the present relevance of a past situation. Thus one of the possible differences between *John has arrived* and *John arrived* is that the former indicates persistence of the result of John's arrival, i.e. that he is still here, whereas the second does not. In answer to the question *is John here yet?* a perfectly reasonable reply would be *yes, he has arrived*, but not *yes, he arrived*.[1] Likewise, the sentence *I have had a bath* implies that the results of my bath (that I am clean, that I don't immediately

---

[1] The reply *yes, he arrived at ten o'clock* is possible, since English requires non-Perfect forms where there is overt time specification.

need another bath) still hold. Of course, this sentence only says that the results do still hold, without giving any indication of the conceptual background to my making this statement: thus Cleopatra may only have uttered such a statement if she had had a bath within the last hour, while for a medieval monk the relevant time-span may rather have been within the last year; in either case, the Perfect is appropriate, since it makes no claims about what constitutes a continuing result, only that there is some continuing result.

The nature of the perfect of result can be examined by comparing translation equivalents across languages where the one uses the Perfect (or, in the absence of a distinct perfect, a past tense) and the other uses the Present of a stative verb (or adjective), i.e. one language expresses this as a (state resulting from a) past action, while the other just expresses it as a present state without any overt mention of how this state came about. Most of the examples seem to concern contrasts where English has a stative adjective or verb, while some other language has a Perfect or other past tense, so that it may be that English overall tends towards the use of the stative Present here to a greater extent than do many other languages.

In Ancient Greek, there are several verbs that are used in the Perfect corresponding to an English stative Present, including *tethnékenai* 'be dead' (Perfect of *thnéiskein* 'die'), *memnēsthai* 'remember' (Perfect of the passive of *mimnéiskein* 'remind'), *hestánai* 'stand' (Perfect of *histánai* 'place (upright)').[1] in Swahili,[2] the Perfect, marked by the prefix *me-* after the subject prefix, can translate an English Perfect, as in *a-me-fika* 'he has arrived', but will often be translated most naturally into English as a stative Present, e.g. *a-me-choka* 'he is tired' (literally 'he has got tired'), *a-me-simama* 'he is standing' (literally 'he has stood up'). In Fante, 'he is tired' is *ɔáfɔ̀ná*, cp. *ɔrìfɔ̀ná* 'he is getting tired' and *ɔábá* 'he has come', i.e. is analysable as *ɔ-á-fɔ̀ná*, literally 'he has got tired'. In Kpelle, 'it is all gone' is translated by *aâ kpɛɛ*, cp. *è kpɛ̀ɛ* 'it got used up' and *aâ ˋkpɛɛ* 'he has finished it'. In Kpelle, even 'see' is expressed as a Perfect, i.e. *aâ ˋkáa* can correspond to either 'he sees it' or 'he has caught sight of it'.[3]

---

[1] Ancient Greek also has some such verbs which lack non-Perfect forms, such as *oîda* 'I know', and correspond to English Presents; these are less telling, since their lack of non-Perfect forms is idiosyncratic within Greek itself. For these and other examples, see Goodwin (1889: 15).

[2] Ashton (1947:37).

[3] The Fante and Kpelle examples are from Welmers (1973: 347–8).

Perfect

In languages with no distinct Perfect, then the Past Tense will be used in such constructions. The normal Russian translation of 'I am tired' is *ja ustal*.[1] This is a form of the verb *ustavat'* (stem *ustaj-*) (Ipfv.), *ustat'* (stem *ustan-*) (Pfv.) 'get tired'. In the Imperfective it appears, for instance, in *ja ustaju* 'I am getting tired, I (habitually) get tired', *ja ustaval* 'I was getting tired, I used to get tired'. In *ja ustal* and *ja ustanu* we have, respectively, the Perfective Past and the Perfective Future of this same verb. Russian does not have a distinct Perfect in the active voice, and *ja ustal* encompasses English 'I have got tired', i.e. 'I am tired', though it can also mean simply 'I got tired', and indeed 'I had got tired', including 'I was tired', given that the Russian Past Tense covers the range of English Past, Present Perfect, and Pluperfect; similarly *ja ustanu* is 'I will get tired', incorporating also 'I will have got tired', i.e. 'I will be tired'.

In Mandarin Chinese, the verbal particle *-le* indicates perfective aspect and relative past time reference (section 4.4). With stative predicates, the force of this particle *-le* is often to indicate a state resulting from some previous situation, as in *dōngxi guì-le* 'things are expensive' (but with the implication that once they were not, i.e. they have become expensive), *tā shēntǐ hǎo-le* 'his health is (has become) good'; these contrast with *dōngxi hěn guì* 'things are very expensive', *tā shēntǐ hěn hǎo* 'his health is very good', where there is no implication that things were ever otherwise. One may also compare the following negative sentences: *tā bù děng* 'he isn't waiting', *tā bù děng-le* 'he is no longer waiting', i.e. he has entered a state of being not waiting.

3.1.2. *Experiential perfect*

The experiential perfect[2] indicates that a given situation has held at least once during some time in the past leading up to the present.

---

[1] Since Russian has no overt copula in the Present Tense, one might think, from the English gloss, that *ustal* is an adjective 'tired', and there is indeed an adjective *ustalyj* 'tired' of which this could, morphologically, be the predicative form. However, further examination shows that the *ustal* of *ja ustal* is not a form of the adjective *ustalyj*; for instance, 'I was tired' still comes out as *ja ustal*, although with an adjectival predicate the Past Tense of the copula is *byl*. In Russian one cannot say **ja byl ustal*. Moreover, the plural is *my ustali*, with the verbal ending *-i*; the adjectival ending *-y* would give **my ustaly*. 'I will be tired' is *ja ustanu*, where *ustanu* can only be a verb.

[2] Other terms found in the literature are 'existential' perfect, 'indefinite' perfect.

A useful illustrative example in English is the distinction between *be* and *go* in sentences like *Bill has been to America* and *Bill has gone to America*, since English here makes an overt distinction between the experiential perfect and the perfect of result. *Bill has gone to America* is perfect of result, and implies that Bill is now in America, or is on his way there, this being the present result of his past action of going to (setting out for) America. In *Bill has been to America*, however, there is no such implication; this sentence says that on at least one occasion (though possibly on more than one) Bill did in fact go to America. In general, however, English does not have a distinct form with experiential perfect meaning. A number of other languages, including most of the more familiar European languages, are like English in not making any systematic distinction between these two senses. However, some languages can and do make the distinction regularly. In Mandarin Chinese,[1] the marker of the Experiential Perfect is the toneless suffix *-guo*.[2] Thus in Chinese we have a contrast between *nǐ chī-le yúchì-le méi-you* 'have you eaten the shark's fin?' and *nǐ chī-guo yúchì méi-you* 'have you ever eaten shark's fin?'. A similar distinction exists in Kpelle.[3] The Perfect of result for 'I have fixed it' would be *ŋaâ ʼkpɛtɛ* (sc. and it works), while the Experiential Perfect would be *ŋà ʼkpɛtɛ* (i.e. I have indeed on one or more occasions fixed it, but it keeps breaking down). The difference between English *he has gone to Monrovia* and *he has been to Monrovia* comes out in the same way, as respectively: *aâ lí Dukɔ̃ɔ* and *à lí Dukɔ̃ɔ*.

In the examples of the experiential perfect given so far, it has been the case that the time during which the situation referred to must have held at least once has included the whole of time up to the present; thus *Bill has been to America* places no restriction on when Bill went to America, other than that it was sometime before the present. It is possible to restrict the period of time by specifying an earlier limit, in addition to the necessary later limit of the present moment, as in *Bill has been to America since the war*, which says that Bill has been to America at least once in the period between the war (earlier limit) and the present moment (later limit).[4]

---

[1] Chao (1968: 251–2).

[2] There is also a suffix *-guò*, usually with fourth tone, indicating completion of an action; apart from the potential tone difference, *-guò* of completed action, but not experiential *-guo*, may be followed by other aspectual markers, e.g. *-le*.　　　　[3] Welmers (1973: 351–2).

[4] With the experiential perfect the requirement of present relevance is still important. Thus Chomsky (1971: 212–13) and McCawley (1971:106–8)

3.1.3. *Perfect of persistent situation*

One use of the English Perfect, indeed one that seems to be characteristic of English, is the use of the Perfect to describe a situation that started in the past but continues (persists) into the present, as in *we've lived here for ten years. I've shopped there for years, I've been waiting for hours.* Many other languages use the present tense here: French *j'attends depuis trois jours*, German *ich warte schon drei Tage*, Russian *ja ždu uže tri dnja* 'I have been waiting for three days'.[1] The use of the Perfect here in English is not entirely surprising, since the situation referred to is both past and present, though it is clear that a language is by no means forced to express such situations in this way, and indeed it seems more typical not to.

3.1.4. *Perfect of recent past*

In many languages, the perfect may be used where the present relevance of the past situation referred to is simply one of temporal closeness, i.e. the past situation is very recent. In English, for instance, the general constraint against combining the Perfect with a specification of time does not hold when the time specification is the adverb *recently* or one of its close synonyms: *I have recently learned that the match is to be postponed, Bill has just (this minute) arrived.* The perfect does not, of course, in general necessarily imply that the past situation is recent, since present relevance does not necessarily imply recentness: the sentence *the Second World War has ended* will be perfectly acceptable to someone who has been on a desert island, cut off from all sources of news since 1944.[2] However, while present relevance does not imply recentness, recentness may be a sufficient condition for present relevance.

The degree of recentness required varies among languages that

note the anomaly of *Einstein has visited Princeton*, with *Einstein* as subject (according to Chomsky) or topic (according to McCawley) of the sentence, given that Einstein is known to be dead. Both Chomsky and McCawley claim that *Princeton has been visited by Einstein* is acceptable, with *Princeton* as subject or topic, given the knowledge that Princeton still exists. The present author's judgement does not agree with theirs on the second sentence, and it seems that the precise conditions are subject to some degree of idiolectal variation.

[1] Such sentences in German and Russian often contain the adverb *schon* (German), *uže* (Russian) 'already'.

[2] Compare McCawley's discussion (1971: 348–50) of what he terms the 'hot news perfect'.

allow the perfect to express recent past time reference. For most speakers of English, only the adverb *recently* and its near synonyms are allowed, while any other specification of past time or period is excluded, i.e. one cannot say **I've been to the dentist this morning* during the afternoon or evening.[1] In Spanish, the use of the Perfect for recent situations is rather wider, so that *la he visto* (Perfect) *esta mañana* would be possible for 'I saw her this morning', said in the afternoon. Gradual relaxation of the degree of recentness required for use of the Perfect seems to have been a key part of the development of the Perfect in many Romance languages to oust the Simple Past completely. In French grammar of the seventeenth century, a rule of thumb, the 'rule of twenty-four hours', was stated,[2] whereby the Perfect could be used for a situation that held not more than twenty-four hours before the present; while the criterion was hardly as rigid as this in practice, the rule does bear some relation to usage of the time. In modern spoken French, Italian, and Romanian, except in certain regional dialects of these languages, the Perfect has completely supplanted the Simple Past; since the Perfect in these languages does not have perfect meaning, the term 'Compound Past' is perhaps preferable to 'Perfect', as in some traditional grammars of these languages. Given that the perfect partakes of both present and past, it is possible for languages to differ over just how present or past their perfect forms are. The development that has taken place in these Romance languages can be seen as a gradual reduction of the presentness of the relevant forms, which finally become purely past.

3.2. Perfect and other aspects

3.2.0. In the majority of those languages where it is formally possible for the perfect/nonperfect distinction to combine freely with other aspectual distinctions, we find that such combinations do in fact occur. There are exceptions, such as Modern Greek, where the Perfect, in any case more restricted in use than in English, for instance, can only

---

[1] The important factor here is whether or not the period referred to as *this morning* is over or not. One can say *I've been to the dentist's today* in the afternoon, even if the visit in fact took place in the morning, since *today* includes the present moment (as well as the morning), and is thus not a specification of past time. But see also footnote 1, page 54.

[2] Lancelot and Arnauld (1660: 103–4), who cite the examples *j'écrivis* (Past Definite) *hier* 'I wrote yesterday', but *j'ai écrit* (Perfect) *ce matin, cette nuit* 'I wrote this morning, last night'.

be formed from Perfective verbs;[1] in Georgian, the Imperfective Perfect is rare, at least for nonstative verbs.[2] In Ancient Greek, the morphology of the Perfect precludes combination with the Aorist/Imperfect aspectual distinction, since different stems are used for the three verb forms, e.g. *élūon* (Imperfect) 'I was loosing, used to loose', *élūsa* (Aorist) 'I loosed', *léluka* (Perfect) 'I have loosed'. But the main point of interest here will be the combinability and resultant meaning of aspectual distinctions that can be combined, such as perfect and progressive in English (*I have been singing*) and Portuguese (*tenho estado trabalhando* 'I have been working'), or Perfect and Imperfective in Bulgarian. At first sight, it may seem contradictory that a verb form can be both perfect and imperfective, or both perfect and progressive (given that progressive is even more restricted than imperfective), but this apparent contradiction is once again due to the tendency to confuse perfect and perfective. The perfect links a present state to a past situation, whether this past situation was an individual event, or a state, or a process not yet completed, so that there is nothing in the definition of the perfect to preclude combination with the imperfective or progressive.[3]

The possible range of meaning of such combinations of aspectual categories can be illustrated by looking at the English Perfect Progressive. If we take first of all the characteristically English use of the Perfect to refer to a persistent situation, i.e. one that continues up to the present time (and may continue beyond), then we find that the distribution of the Progressive and non-Progressive forms is essentially the same as in the Present Tense: the non-Progressive form must be used with stative verbs (**I have been knowing him for a long time*), while other verbs, unless habitual, will normally be in the Progressive (*I have been speaking for ages*). With the experiential perfect, it is quite possible for the situation in which we are interested to be an ongoing process, as in *have you ever been watching television when the tube has exploded?* Similarly with the perfect of recent past, as in *the police have recently been keeping my neighbour under observation*, or *I have just this minute been talking to my solicitor*. More generally, the Perfect Progressive combines the possible meanings of the Perfect with the possible meanings of the Progressive.[4]

---

[1] Thus corresponding to *éxo féri* (Pfv.) 'I have carried' there is no **éxo férni* (Ipfv.).   [2] Vogt (1971: 193).

[3] In Bulgarian, the Imperfective Perfect is also possible given the unmarkedness of the Imperfective vis-à-vis the Perfective; see chapter 6.

[4] Compare the discussion in Leech (1971: 44–7).

In the discussion of Russian *ja ustal* 'I am tired' or 'I got tired' towards the end of section 3.1.1, we noted that Russian often uses the Perfective to correspond to explicitly perfect forms in languages that have such forms, although Russian has in fact no distinct perfect forms.[1] However, the Russian Imperfective is by no means incompatible with perfect meaning. Some instances of the Imperfective allowing perfect meaning follow from the unmarkedness of the Russian Imperfective (chapter 6), but not all. For instance, if I visit a friend and see his house half-whitewashed, and him sitting in his garden resting, then I may say, in English, *I see you've been whitewashing the house*: the present half-whitewashed state of the house is the result of my friend's having been occupied in the task of whitewashing it, whence the Perfect Progressive. If I were to say in Russian, using the Perfective, *vy pobelili dom*, then this could only imply that the whitewashing was already complete, i.e. 'you've whitewashed the house', and in the situation described above this would simply be untrue. In fact, in such a case in Russian one could use the (Imperfective) Present, to describe a process which, at the present moment, is not yet complete, i.e. *vy belite dom*; without a more elaborate paraphrase there is no way of conveying the idea contained in the English Progressive Perfect of a situation that has been interrupted but whose completed portion has present results. Similarly, there are cases where English will use the Perfect but Russian will use the Imperfective where the English Perfect refers to a habitual situation, as in *oni prodolžajut pol'zovat'sja starymi metodami, kotorye uže ne raz opravdyvali* (Ipfv.) *sebja* 'they continue to use the old methods, which have already on many occasions justified themselves'. Corresponding to the English Perfect, then, one finds both Perfective and Imperfective in Russian, just as one finds both aspects corresponding to English non-Perfect forms. The perfect/nonperfect opposition is different from the perfective/imperfective opposition.

There does still, however, remain the generalisation that there are some languages, like Modern Greek, where the perfect is restricted to perfective aspect, while there are apparently none where the perfect is restricted to imperfective aspect, i.e. there is a more natural relationship between perfect and perfective than between perfect and imperfective. If we look again at the meaning of the perfect and of the perfective/

---

[1] This applies strictly only to the active voice; for the passive, see section 4.6. For a recent discussion of Russian Perfectives with perfect meaning, see Lönngren (1973).

imperfective opposition, the reason for this frequent, but by no means obligatory, relation becomes clear: the perfect looks at a situation in terms of its consequences, and while it is possible for an incomplete situation to have consequences, it is much more likely that consequences will be consequences of a situation that has been brought to completion, i.e. of a situation that is likely to be described by means of the perfective.

3.3. **Prospective aspect**

The perfect is retrospective, in that it establishes a relation between a state at one time and a situation at an earlier time. If languages were completely symmetrical, one might equally well expect to find prospective forms, where a state is related to some subsequent situation, for instance where someone is in a state of being about to do something. Many languages do have means of giving overt expression to prospective meaning, though in some languages it is difficult to find exact equivalents without going into long periphrases. As noted in the Introduction, languages are not in fact symmetrical about the axis of present time, so that it should not be surprising that there is no direct correspondence between forms with perfect meaning and forms with prospective meaning.

Typical English expressions of prospective meaning are the constructions *to be going to, to be about to, to be on the point of*, as in *the ship is about to sail, the ship is on the point of sailing* – both of which describe the ship's present state relative to some future event, with these constructions an imminently future event – and *the ship is going to sail*, where there is again a present state related to a future event, but here without any implication of imminent futurity.[1] It is important to appreciate the difference between these expressions of prospective meaning and expressions of straight future time reference, e.g. between *Bill is going to throw himself off the cliff* and *Bill will throw himself off the cliff*. If we imagine a situation where someone says one of these two sentences, and then Bill is in fact prevented from throwing himself off the cliff, then if the speaker said *Bill will throw himself off the cliff*, he was wrong, his prediction was not borne out. If, however, he said *Bill is going to throw himself off the cliff*, then he was not necessarily wrong,

---

[1] Compare the examples quoted by Leech (1971: 56): *I'm going to be a policeman when I grow up; if Winterbottom's calculations are correct, this planet is going to burn itself out 200,000,000 years from now*. Note that here, unlike in the Perfect, it is possible to specify the time at which the future situation will occur.

since all he was alluding to was Bill's intention to throw himself off the cliff, i.e. to the already present seeds of some future situation, which future situation might well be prevented from coming about by intervening factors. Indeed, *Bill is going to throw himself off the cliff* might well be shouted as a warning to some third party to prevent the future situation from coming about.

In Russian, for instance, it is very difficult to give an adequate translation of an English prospective of this type, without adding or subtracting some element of meaning. Thus one translation of *I am going to kill you* would be *ja sobirajus' ubit' tebja*, literally 'I intend to kill you', but this does add an element of intention which is not necessarily present in the English prospective forms. This construction could not be used as the Russian translation of *there are going to be apples for pudding*, where the apples are presumably not intending to be eaten for pudding, and in Russian one can only use the ordinary Future Tense: *budut jabloki na tret'e* 'there will be apples for pudding'. Sometimes Russian uses *dolžen* 'must' in such constructions, e.g. *poezd dolžen prijti v sem' časov* 'the train is going to arrive at seven o'clock', but again the Russian is not an exact equivalent of the English, and a better gloss might be 'the train is due to arrive at seven o'clock'.

4

Aspect and tense

4.0. So far, we have been emphasising the difference between tense and aspect, particularly in so far as traditional grammatical terminology does not always rigorously distinguish the two parameters, which can lead to confusion in discussing either aspect or tense in its own right. However, at various points it has been noted that aspect and tense do sometimes impinge on one another, and it is now time to examine more systematically some of the relationships between aspect and tense in various languages.

4.1. Perfective, present, and future

Since the present tense is essentially used to describe, rather than to narrate, it is essentially imperfective, either continuous or habitual, and not perfective. In this section we shall look at perfective presents in various languages, investigating the meanings associated with this apparently contradictory combination of categories.

In languages where the basic tense distinction is between past and non-past, we have strictly speaking not the possibility of a perfective present, but rather of a perfective non-past, i.e. of the perfective of the present-future. Since the present is primarily a tense of description, it is quite natural for the perfective non-past to have as one of its meaning that of a perfective future. Various stages of this development of perfective non-past to perfective future can be seen in different Indo-European (especially Slavonic) and non-Indo-European languages. In Hungarian, where the aspectual significance of the verbal prefixes is rather weakly developed, although they tend to give the verb perfective meaning, there is a tendency for the nonpast of such prefixed verbs to have future meaning.[1] In the East and West Slavonic languages (including Russian, Polish, Czech, but not Bulgarian or Serbo-Croatian), and

[1] Majtinskaja (1959: 181).

66

also in Georgian, the development is more complete, so that the Perfective non-Past is primarily a future tense, a point to which we shall return in greater detail below; it is paralleled by a new periphrastic formation for the Imperfective Future.[1] With nonderived verbs of motion in Czech, a further development has taken place whereby the earlier Perfective non-Past has become a Future Tense irrespective of aspect, i.e. a development from Perfective non-Past to Perfective Future to Future. In the Past Tense, *šel* 'went' is Imperfective, and *pošel* Perfective. But in the non-Past, the difference between *jdu* and *půjdu* (for *po+jdu*) is not aspectual (as is the case with Russian *idu*, Imperfective Present, versus *pojdu*, Perfective Future), but purely temporal, i.e. *jdu* 'I go, am going', *půjdu* 'I shall go, shall have gone, shall be going'. With these verbs of motion Czech has no specifically Imperfective Future *budu jít to parallel Russian *budu idti* 'I shall be going, shall go (Ipfv.)', although this is how Imperfective Futures of other verbs are formed in Czech too, e.g. *budu číst* 'I shall be reading, shall read (Ipfv.)'. One explanation of the etymology of the Ancient Greek aspectually neutral Future Tense, e.g. *grápsō* 'I shall write, shall be writing', would derive this too from the Aorist (i.e. perfective) stem of the verb, cp. the Aorist *égrapsa* 'I wrote'.[2]

In the light of this expected restriction of the perfective nonpast to future tense, it is worth looking in some detail at those languages where the perfective present is not primarily a future tense (e.g. South Slavonic) and also at individual usages in some of the languages that normally have the expected development, but sometimes have a perfective non-past that seems to parallel the imperfective present rather than the imperfective future (where this is a distinct form from the imperfective present). The uses of the Perfective Present in South Slavonic involve cases where the Present Tense is used in ways that are not strictly referring to the present moment.

One characteristic of the South Slavonic languages, found in its fullest form in Bulgarian, though also to a certain extent in Serbo-Croatian, for instance, is the loss of the Infinitive and its replacement by a subordinate clause with the conjunction *da* and the Present Tense

---

[1] In the South Slavonic languages, including Bulgarian and Serbo-Croatian, there is a periphrastic Future for both aspects, so that the Perfective Present is not a Future Tense, as it is in East and West Slavonic; the Perfective Present in South Slavonic is discussed further below.

[2] Kuryłowicz (1964: 115).

(though without any necessary reference to present time, any more than there is with the Infinitive in languages like English or Russian that have an Infinitive). The Infinitive can distinguish aspect in Russian, where we have the Imperfective in *ja mogu letat'* 'I can fly', but the Perfective in *ja xoču kupit' knigu* 'I want to buy a book'. If we translate these sentences into Bulgarian, we must replace the Infinitive by the Present Tense, but since there is not actual reference to present time, the aspectual opposition may and must be retained: *moga da letja* (Ipfv.), literally 'I-can that I-fly (Ipfv.)', versus *iskam da kupja* (Pfv.) *kniga*, literally 'I-want that I-buy book'. If the main verbs are put into the Past Tense, there is no change in the form of the subordinate verb: *možax da letja* 'I could fly', *iskax da kupja kniga* 'I wanted to buy a book'.

In English, a sentence like *he comes here* on its own, in present meaning, will normally be interpreted with habitual meaning, since if the reference were to an action going on at the present moment it would have to be *he is coming here*, i.e. Progressive. However, in a context where *he comes here* does not have present time reference, then perfective meaning is a possible interpretation, as in a subordinate clause of time, e.g. *when he comes here, I'll tell him*, since here the verb *comes* refers to a future action. Different languages differ as to whether or not they require overt specification of futurity in such temporal clauses; contrast with the English sentence above its French translation: *quand il viendra* (Future) *ici, je le lui dirai*, and also with its Russian translation: *kogda on pridet* (Future), *ja emu skažu*. Bulgarian and Serbo-Croatian in such sentences are like English rather than French or Russian, and have the Present in the temporal clause, as in Bulgarian *sled kato svərša* (Pfv. Present) *tazi rabota, šte otida* (Pfv. Future) *na selo* 'when I finish this work, I shall go to the country'.

At this point, an apparent weakness of the comparison between languages like English and Bulgarian on the one hand and French and Russian on the other, especially between Bulgarian and Russian, may strike the reader. Morphologically, Russian *pridet* in the example quoted above is a Perfective non-Past, cp. the Imperfective Present *idet* 'he-goes'. The same is true, morphologically, of Bulgarian *svərša*, although given the existence of a separate Perfective Future in Bulgarian (with *šte*) *svərša* is specifically Perfective Present rather than the less specific Perfective non-Past. Given the parallelism of morphological formation between the forms used in Bulgarian and Russian, and the fact that both are used equally in temporal clauses with future reference, it may seem casuistic to speak in the one case (Bulgarian) of a Perfective Present and in the other (Russian) of a Perfective Future, since the data provide no evidence for such a distinction. However, the different functions of the morphologically parallel Bulgarian and Russian forms can be identified by comparing sentences where the verb in the subordinate clause is Imperfective, rather than Perfective, because here Bulgarian and Russian have quite different morphological expressions of the Imperfective Future: in Bulgarian the particle *šte* with the Imperfective Present, in Russian *budu* with the Imperfective Infinitive. And in such sentences we find a clear distinction between Bulgarian, with the Imperfective Present as in English, and Russian, with the Imperfective Future as in French: Bulgarian *az kato peja* (Ipfv. Present), *ti šte plačeš*, Russian *kogda ja budu pet'* (Ipfv. Future), *ty budeš' plakat'*, French *quand je chanterai* (Future) *tu pleureras*, English *when I am singing* (Present) *you will be crying*. Thus the comparison with corresponding Imperfectives confirms the distinction between Bulgarian with the Present Tense in what is strictly not present time reference (as in English), and Russian with the Future Tense (as in French), despite the apparent morphological parallelism between Perfective Present in Bulgarian and Perfective Future in Russian.

Another function of the Perfective Present in Bulgarian is in the narrative Present, i.e. when the Present Tense is used with past meaning as a narrative technique with retention of the aspectual distinctions usual in the Past Tense. This use of the Perfective Present is discussed in greater detail in section 4.3.

Finally, in Bulgarian the Perfective Present may be used with habitual meaning, or rather is one of the possible means of expressing habituality, where the habituality involved is that of a situation which would in itself, as a single instance, be treated as perfective; i.e. the Present Tense is used to express a habitual situation by presenting one instance to exemplify the recurrent situation, as in:[1] *spoglednat* (Pfv. Present) *se, pousmixnat* (Pfv. Present) *devojki, ponadevat* (Pfv. Present) *zarumeni lica* . . . 'the girls look at one another, smile at one another, incline their reddened faces . . .'. The sense is not, however, that this is what they are doing at the present moment, but rather that this is what happens whenever a certain set of circumstances holds (and, indeed, it is quite likely that this particular set of circumstances does not hold precisely

---

[1] This example is cited by Andrejczin (1938: 32).

at the present moment). This function of the Perfective Present is paralleled by the use of the Perfective Imperfect in Bulgarian to indicate a habitual perfective situation in past time (see section 1.2.1.1).

With this habitual use of the Perfective Present, it may seem once again that Russian has the same phenomenon as Bulgarian, since Russian too has a similar use of the Perfective non-Past with habitual meaning, and indeed in this usage the Perfective non-Past usually occurs in conjunction with the Imperfective Present, i.e. abstracting away from the aspectual differences it would appear that we are here dealing with a Perfective Present in Russian. This usage is very common with past time reference, the actual past time being marked by temporal adverbials, the verb form *byvalo* 'it used to be (the case that . . .)', or simply by context, as in the following example from Turgenev:[1]

Byvalo, sidit (Ipfv.) . . . i smotrit (Ipfv.) na Irinu . . . a ona kak budto serditsja (Ipfv.), kak budto skučaet (Ipfv.), vstanet (Pfv.), projdetsja (Pfv.) po komnate, xolodno posmotrit (Pfv.) na nego, požmet (Pfv.) plečom.
It used to happen that he would sit (Ipfv.) . . . and gaze (Ipfv.) at Irina . . . and would seem to be angry (Ipfv.), to be bored (Ipfv.), she would get up (Pfv.), walk about (Pfv.) the room, look (Pfv.) coldly at him, shrug (Pfv.) her shoulders.

Here, the Imperfective forms describe the background states of each occurrence of this series of events, while the actual events are expressed by Perfective forms, the tenses being the Imperfective Present and the Perfective non-Past. However, as will be discussed in greater detail in section 4.3, there is in current usage a tendency for this aspectual distinction to be expressed rather by the difference between the Imperfective Future (i.e. *budu* with the Infinitive) and the Perfective non-Past (Future); it is only the fact that the Perfective non-Past is a Perfective Future that explains the current movement towards using the Imperfective Future rather than the Imperfective Present in such constructions.

Despite the formal parallelism between the Perfective Present in Bulgarian (and similar languages, such as Serbo-Croatian) and the Perfective non-Past in Russian (and similar languages, such as Czech and Polish), it emerges that the latter is primarily a future tense, and not a present tense, while apparent instances of its use as a present tense are to be treated as remnants, as anomalies within the synchronic system. Given the historical development from a Perfective non-Past, the existence of such relicts of earlier usage is not surprising. In Georgian,

[1] Cited by Borras and Christian (1971: 122).

as in Russian, the Perfective non-Past is now primarily a future tense, although there are perhaps rather more remnants of earlier usage where the Perfective non-Past parallels exactly the Imperfective Present, as in the maintenance of aspectual distinctions in the narrative Present (section 4.3), although the absence in Georgian of any specifically Imperfective Future should also be noted as a conditioning factor: Georgian has in fact an Imperfective non-Past and a Perfective non-Past, the former being rather freely present or future, the latter future except in certain special usages (in particular the narrative and habitual Present) with overt indication of its unusual time reference.

Summarising the relation between aspect and tense in Russian, we can say that there is a Present Tense which is Imperfective, a Past Tense with an Imperfective/Perfective opposition, and a Future Tense with an Imperfective/Perfective opposition. Morphologically, the Imperfective Future rather falls outside the system, being periphrastic, while the morphological parallelism is rather between the Imperfective Present and the Perfective Future. The morphology, together with some individual usages of the Perfective Future, suggest an earlier stage where there was just one non-Past Tense with an Imperfective/Perfective aspectual distinction, but this is no longer true of the modern language, where restrictions on the compatibility of Present and Perfective have led to the Perfective non-Past becoming specifically a Perfective Future.[1]

4.2. Aspectual distinctions restricted to certain tenses

One of the most interesting relationships between aspect and tense, from the viewpoint of language as a functional system, occurs when an aspectual distinction is restricted to one or more tenses, rather than operating across the board, independently of tense. It appears that the tense that most often evinces aspectual distinctions is the past tense. Thus in many Indo-European languages, and also in Georgian, the difference between the Aorist and the Imperfect exists only in the Past Tense, and there is no corresponding distinction in other tenses: thus the distinction between Spanish *hablé* 'I spoke' and *hablaba* 'I was speaking, used to speak', Latin *veni* 'I came' and *veniebam* 'I was coming, used to come', Bulgarian *broix* 'I counted' and *brojax* 'I was counting, used to count', Georgian (*da*)*çere* 'you wrote' and *çerdi* 'you

---

[1] For a different analysis of the Russian Perfective non-Past, arguing that it is not a future tense, see Ferrell (1953).

were writing, used to write' is not paralleled by any comparable distinction in the Present or Future, or in the nonfinite forms of the verb (e.g. infinitives and participles, except in certain cases where these are explicitly Past Tense). In these cases the aspectual distinction is essentially between perfective meaning on the one hand and imperfective meaning on the other. Given that this is the basic distinction, it is not surprising from a functional viewpoint that there should be no similar distinction in the present, since the present, as an essentially descriptive tense, can normally only be of imperfective meaning. In contrasting past and present tense, it therefore becomes clearer why there should be a greater need for this particular aspectual distinction in the past than in the present. One still needs an explanation for why so many languages would make an explicit aspectual distinction in the past. Correlations between aspect and time reference in a number of African languages, among others,[1] suggest that the most typical usages of verbs in the present tense are those denoting actions in progress or states (i.e. with continuous, or continuous and habitual meaning), whereas in the past the most typical usages of verbs, especially nonstative verbs, are those with perfective meaning. If we take it that it is most natural for a past tense verb to have perfective meaning, then it is natural for a language to seek some other means of expressing a past tense that does not indicate a single complete action, and it is here that the Imperfect/Aorist distinction enters. In fact, the Imperfect expresses in past tense an aspectual value that is more typical of the present. In traditional Indo-European linguistics, the Imperfect is often characterised as the 'Present in the Past', which captures the above observation that the Imperfect expresses a typically present tense aspectual value in the past tense.

However, in some languages we find other aspectual distinctions made in the past tense but not in other tenses, suggesting that it may well be a general characteristic of human languages to resort to greater aspectual differentiation in the past than in other tenses. Thus the English periphrastic Habitual with *used to* has no corresponding form in other tenses. Similarly, the Slavonic Habitual in -*v*- occurs most typically in the Past Tense, and in some languages, such as Russian, is virtually restricted to Past Tense, apart from a few isolated verbs like *byvat'* 'be (habitually)'. Presumably the greater potential aspectual range of the past tense is an impetus towards greater aspectual differentiation in this tense. With these Habituals, unlike the most typical

[1] For the details, see section 4.5.

Indo-European Imperfects and Aorists, there is no morphological reason why the aspectual distinction should be restricted to only the one tense.

Thus an explicit perfective, distinct from the imperfective, is most common in the past tense, and least common in the present tense. Of course, if the tense distinction is past versus nonpast, rather than past versus future, then it is possible for there to be a perfective non-past, with basically future meaning, as in Russian. Apart from the past, where the perfective is commonest, and the present, where it is rarest, there does not seem to be any general principle as to where aspectual distinctions will next manifest themselves, since the remaining categories (future tense, and nonfinite forms like infinitives and participles) seem equally susceptible to aspectual differentiation, although in Ancient Greek we find the aspectual distinction between Aorist and Imperfect carried over to the various nonfinite forms, but not to the Future. Since the future is generally rather poorly differentiated as a tense distinct from the present in many European languages, this may be the reason for the absence of as well-marked an aspectual distinction in this tense; compare the absence in Italian, but not in Spanish, of a Future Progressive (Italian *starò scrivendo*, Spanish *estaré escribiendo* 'I shall be writing'), although there is no morphological reason for the absence of *starò scrivendo* in Italian.

4.3. Narrative present

One interesting facet of the general problem of the relation between tense and aspect can be studied by examining cases where languages use one tense in place of another, for instance in the narrative present, where the present tense is used to refer to a past situation. A simple English example would be the use of *I'm sitting on the verandah when up comes Joe and says . . .* rather than *I was sitting on the verandah when up came Joe and said . . .*, though this use of the Present is perhaps rather less common in English than in other European languages. Since the English Progressive is not tied to any one tense, there is no problem with aspect in the narrative Present, the difference between Progressive and non-Progressive being retained, or rather retainable, in the displaced version. This is not true of French, for instance, where the difference between perfective and imperfective meaning is only maintained overtly in the Past Tense, by the difference between Past Definite and Imperfect. Thus the aspect distinction in the Past Tense version is lost when we use the narrative Present:

(i) in Past Tense
Un homme *s'amenait* (Imperfect) sur la route, il *conduisait* (Imperfect) trois moutons. Il *aperçut* (Past Definite) l'âne chargé et *dit* (Past Definite) . . .
(ii) in Present Tense
Un homme *s'amène* sur la route, il *conduit* trois moutons. Il *aperçoit* l'âne chargé et *dit* . . .
A man *was/is walking* along the road, he *was/is leading* three sheep. He *saw/sees* the laden donkey and *said/says* . . .

In French, then, and likewise in other Romance languages, the morphological restriction of overt aspect differentiation to the Past Tense means that a priori there can be no aspect distinction in the narrative Present. In languages that do have a morphological aspect distinction in the non-past tenses too, there are two logical possibilities: either the aspect difference of the past will be retained, even if this means using morphological forms (like the Perfective non-Past in Georgian) that are normally restricted to future time reference; or the illusion of presentness (description rather than narration) will be completed by neutralising the aspect distinction.[1]

In Georgian, although the Perfective non-Past usually has future meaning, in the narrative Present it is used to parallel the Imperfective Present, retaining the aspect distinction; thus the Perfective non-Past corresponds to the Perfective (typically Aorist) Past, the Imperfective Present to the Imperfective (typically Imperfect) Past:[2]

(i) in Past Tense
Gzaze erti ḳaci *midioda* (Ipfv. Imperfect), sami cxvari *mihqavda* (Ipfv. Imperfect), *dainaxa* (Pfv. Aorist) daḳidebuli ʒori da *tkva* (Pfv. Aorist) . . .
(ii) in Present Tense
Gzaze erti ḳaci *midis* (Ipfv. Present), sami cxvari *mihqavs* (Ipfv. Present), *dainaxavs* (Pfv. Present) daḳidebul ʒors da *iṭqvis* (Pfv. Present) . . .
A man *was/is going* along the road, he *was/is leading* three sheep, he *saw/sees* the laden donkey and *said/says* . . .

In Georgian, then, although the Perfective of the Present usually has future meaning, this does not prevent the use of this form in the narrative Present.

In Bulgarian, although there is a Perfective Present that does not

---

[1] Quite generally, in languages that have a narrative Present, we find different choices as to how present and how past this form behaves. Thus in Latin, in the sequence of tenses, the narrative Present (historic Present) may be treated either as a primary (i.e. non-Past) or as a historic (i.e. Past) tense (Gildersleeve and Lodge 1895: 314–17).

[2] Vogt (1971: 181–2).

have specifically future meaning, yet still the more usual construction in the narrative Present is to lose the aspect difference, using the Imperfective to correspond to Past Tense forms irrespective of aspect (Perfective versus Imperfective, Aorist versus Imperfect), and completing the illusion of presentness:[1]

(i) in Past Tense
Carja *spjaše* (Ipfv. Imperfect)... *Čukna* (Pfv. Aorist) djado Ivan—nikoj ne mu se *obadi* (Pfv. Aorist). *Trəgna* (Pfv. Aorist) po belija kaldarəm...
(ii) in Present Tense
Carja *spi* (Ipfv. Present)... *Čuka* (Ipfv. Present) djado Ivan—nikoj ne mu se *obadžda* (Ipfv. Present). *Trəgva* (Ipfv. Present) po belija kaldarəm...
The King *was/is sleeping*... Old Ivan *knocked/knocks*—no-one *answered/answers*. He *set/sets off* along the white pavement...

However, it is also possible to maintain the aspect distinction between Perfective and Imperfective in the narrative Present, corresponding to Perfective Past (usually Aorist) and Imperfective Past (usually Imperfect), respectively.[2]

At the other extreme we find Russian. Here, the Perfective non-Past has been preempted as a future tense, so that in the narrative Present only the Imperfective Present may be used, as in the following example from Aksenov:[3]

(i) in Past Tense
Vdrug naša polutorka *ostanovilas'* (Pfv.). Vperedi doroga *byla* (Ipfv.) pusta. Tol'ko daleko-daleko kakoj-to odinokij malen'kij soldatik *stojal* (Ipfv.) i *smotrel* (Ipfv.) v našu storonu. Staršina *spal* (Ipfv.). My s Saškoj *soskočili* (Pfv.) na dorogu...
(ii) in Present Tense
Vdrug naša polutorka *ostanavlivaetsja* (Ipfv.). Vperedi doroga pusta. Tol'ko daleko-daleko kakoj-to odinokij malen'kij soldatik *stoit* (Ipfv.) i *smotrit* (Ipfv.) v našu storonu. Staršina *spit* (Ipfv.). My s Saškoj *soskakivaem* (Ipfv.) na dorogu...
Suddenly our one-and-a-half-tonner *stopped/stops*. The road ahead *was/is* empty. Only way in the distance a lonely small soldier *stood/stands* and *looked/looks* in our direction. The sergeant-major *was/is sleeping*. Sashka and I *jumped/jump down* onto the road...

---

[1] This example is cited by Andrejczin (1938: 32).
[2] M. Ivić informs me that the use of the Serbo-Croatian narrative Present is similar to that of Bulgarian in this respect: either the aspect distinction is lost in favour of the Imperfective, or it may be retained.
[3] Cited by Forsyth (1970: 151); the Past Tense version is mine.

There is no possibility of using the Perfective non-Past in such a sentence.

However, there is another narrative usage of the Present Tense in Russian, with habitual meaning: a recurrent sequence of events is narrated as if it were a single sequence, i.e. one instance stands for the whole pattern. Here, it is usual to maintain the aspectual distinction: corresponding to an Imperfective Past we have the Imperfective Present, while corresponding to the Perfective Past we have the Perfective non-Past, this time devoid of future meaning. In the following example from Sholokhov,[1] we have first the appropriate Past Tense forms for describing one individual occurrence of the sequence in question, then the narrative use of the Present:

(i) in Past Tense
(Levuju ruku otorvalo po lokot', no i odnoj krutil Aleksej cigarki iskusno i bez promaxa:) *prižal* (Pfv.) kiset k vypuklomu zaslonu grudi, zubami *otorval* (Pfv.) nužnyj kločok bumagi, *sognul* (Pfv.) ego želobkom, *nagreb* (Pfv.) tabaku i neulovimo *povel* (Pfv.) pal'cami, skručivaja. Ne *uspel* (Pfv.) čelovek ogljanut'-sja, a Aleksej, pomargivaja, uže *ževal* (Ipfv.) gotovuju cigarku i *prosil* (Ipfv.) ogon'ku.

(ii) in Present Tense
(Levuju ruku otorvalo po lokot', no i odnoj krutit Aleksej cigarki iskusno i bez promaxa:) *prižmet* (Pfv.) kiset k vypuklomu zaslonu grudi, zubami *otorvet* (Pfv.) nužnyj kločok bumagi, *sognet* (Pfv.) ego želobkom, *nagrebet* (Pfv.) tabaku i neulovimo *povedet* (Pfv.) pal'cami, skručivaja. Ne *uspeet* (Pfv.) čelovek ogljanut'sja, a Aleksej, pomargivaja, uže *žuet* (Ipfv.) gotovuju cigarku i *prosit* (Ipfv.) ogon'ku.

(His left arm had been cut off at the elbow, but even with one Aleksey could roll cigarettes skilfully and without a slip:) He *would press* his tobacco-pouch to his bulging chest, *tear off* the required amount of paper with his teeth, *bend* it into a trough, *scoop up* some tobacco and *roll* it up with dexterous finger movements. One *had no time* to turn around before Aleksey *was already chewing* the finished cigarette, blinking, and *asking* for a light.

In such constructions, Bulgarian behaves like Russian, despite the usual difference between the Bulgarian Perfective Present and the Russian Perfective Future.[2]

---

[1] Cited by Forsyth (1970: 181); the Past Tense version is again mine.

[2] For Russian, there is some evidence that the pure aspectual (rather than combined tense and aspect) opposition between Imperfective Present and Perfective non-Past is exceptional within the general system. Forsyth (1970: 183) notes that in the habitual narrative Present, one occasionally finds the Imperfective Future, rather than the Imperfective Present. In other words, given that in perfective meaning we have the Perfective non-Past, which in Russian is a Perfective Future, the natural tendency is to use as the corresponding Imperfective the Imperfective Future.

Having looked at a number of other languages, we may now return to the interaction of aspect and tense in the English narrative Present. As noted above, in English the non-Progressive Present of nonstative verbs tends to be restricted to expression of habitual actions. Another use of this non-Progressive Present is in the historic Present, where the aspect distinction Progressive/non-Progressive of the Past is retained. A similar use of the non-Progressive Present is what may be called the commentary use of the Present, as in providing a commentary for a film, a football match, or a horse-race (simultaneous narration). Here, although we are in present time, the structure of the communication is that of a narrative. This characteristic structure is reflected in the possibility of using the non-Progressive Present to refer to complete actions, i.e. to maintain an aspect distinction just as one would in the Past Tense, the only difference being that here the maintenance of the distinction is optional, since as in the Present Tense generally the Progressive can be used for all nonhabitual actions. Thus a film commentary might run:

Now the villain seizes the heroine, now they drive off towards the railway track, now he forces her out of the car, now he ties her to the track, while all the time the train is getting nearer.

(All verb forms except the last are non-Progressive.) Equally, the commentary could have been given throughout in the Progressive form:

Now the villain is seizing the heroine, now they're driving off towards the railway track, now he's forcing her out of the car, now he's tying her to the track, while all the time the train is getting nearer.

One factor influencing the choice between the two possibilities is that the non-Progressive is favoured when a rapid series of events has to be commented on as they are happening.[1]

The usages noted so far in this section have typically shifted the tense (e.g. present for past), and either shifted aspect in accordance with normal usage in the present, or retained aspect in accordance with the distinction between description and narration. Another logical possibility would be to retain the tense, but shift aspect, for instance to lose aspect distinctions in the past tense, just as if the whole had been shifted into the present, with the typical present aspectual distinctions, or lack of distinctions. This may seem a particularly complex set of shifts, but it

[1] Compare Leech (1971: 15).

is apparently quite frequent in contemporary French literary style to make use of the Imparfait pittoresque (picturesque Imperfect), which has just this effect:[1]

'Ce n'est rien', *dit-il* (Past Definite) . . . Puis, au milieu du pansement, il *s'interrompait* (Imperfect) pour s'écrier: 'Coup double! tous les deux roides morts! . . . C'est le curé qui va rire . . . Coup double! Ah! voici enfin cette petite tortue de Chalina.' Orso ne *répondait* (Imperfect) pas. Il était pâle comme un mort et tremblait de tous ses membres.
'It's nothing', *he said* (Past Definite) . . . Then, in the middle of bandaging, he *interrupted himself* (Imperfect) to shout: 'Double hit! Both of them stiff as corpses! . . . It's the vicar who's going to laugh . . . Double hit! Ah! Here's that little tortoise Chalina at last.' Orso *didn't reply* (Imperfect). He was pale as a corpse and trembling in every limb.

Here, the Imperfects *s'interrompait* and *répondait* are used as if the narrative had been transposed into the Present Tense.

4.4. Combined tense/aspect oppositions

In written Arabic,[2] there are two sets of forms, traditionally referred to variously as aspects, tenses, or states, and distinguished either as Perfect and Imperfect, or as Perfective and Imperfective. Here the terms Perfective and Imperfective will be used, although the meanings of the terms are different from those used in Slavonic linguistics and elsewhere in this book, as will become apparent below.

We may start with the function of the Perfective and Imperfective where the rest of the sentence contains no overt specification of time reference (e.g. no temporal adverbs). Here the Perfective is interpreted with perfective and past meaning, while the Imperfective is interpreted with imperfective and present meaning:

Jalasū (Pfv.) ʕalā 'l- bābi.
They-sat-down at   the door.
Ɂallāhu yaʕlamu (Ipfv.)   bi-   mā   taʕmalūna (Ipfv.).
God   he-know   about what you-do.
God knows what you are doing.

On the basis of these two examples, we might hypothesise either that the basic distinction is one of tense (with the aspectual difference in this

[1] Imbs (1960: 92–3): the example is from Mérimée.
[2] The examples and commentary in this section are based mainly on Wright (1898: 1–24). For a recent discussion of the history of the Arabic forms, with comparison with other Semitic languages (especially Akkadian), see Kuryłowicz (1973).

pair being due to chance) or one of aspect (with the time reference difference being a result of preferred interpretations of the aspects). Further investigation reveals that neither of these is true.

The following example introduces a further use of the Imperfective:

> Fa 'llāhu yaḥkumu (Ipfv.) bayna   -hum yawma 'l-qiyāmiti.
> but God he-judge   between them day   the resurrection
> But God will judge between them on the Day of Resurrection.

Given our knowledge that the Day of Resurrection is to take place, or at least so it is claimed, at some time in the future, the verbal form in this sentence has future time reference. However the sentence is not (or at least, not necessarily) interpreted as having imperfective meaning, indeed it could well correspond to a sentence in a Slavonic language with Perfective Aspect. So the difference between the Arabic Perfective and Imperfective cannot be purely one of aspect.

A further complication is introduced by inclusion of subordinate clauses, as in:

> ʔajīʔu (Ipfv.)   -ka   ʔidā 'ḥmarra (Pfv.)   'l- busru.
> I-come   to-you when it-ripen   the unripe-date
> I shall come to you when the unripe date ripens (shall ripen).

The Imperfective *ʔajīʔu* in isolation would be taken as referring to present time, but the presence of the subordinate temporal clause functions as a temporal adverbial forcing at least a preference for an interpretation with future reference, i.e. 'I shall come'. But the interpretation of the Perfective *'ḥmarra* (citation form *ʔaḥmarra*) is not, as predicted on the hypothesis that the Perfective/Imperfective opposition is purely one of tense, with past time reference, but rather with future time reference (i.e. the date has not yet ripened). However, what is important is not the absolute time reference of this verb, but its relative time reference, since what it indicates is that the ripening of the date will precede my coming to you. So one might still conclude that the difference between the Perfective and the Imperfective is one of relative tense. This might seem to be further corroborated by the use of the Imperfective in purpose clauses, since clearly the fulfilment of the purpose must follow (be relative future with respect to) the action designed to carry out that purpose:

> ʔarsala (Pfv.)   yuʕlimu (Ipfv.)   -hu bi-   ðālika.
> he-sent   he-inform   him about this
> He sent (someone) in order to inform him about this.

The Subjunctive, Jussive, and Imperative moods, all of which have relative future time reference, exist only in the Imperfective, e.g. *ḥattā taḥḍura* (Subjunctive) *ʔuxtī* 'until my sister should come', *yaktub* (Jussive) 'may he write', *ʔuktub* (Imperative) 'write!' Apparently, the Perfective indicates relative past time, the Imperfective relative nonpast (present or future) time.

It was noted above that the Imperfective, taken in isolation, is interpreted as referring to the present, although it can be interpreted as referring to the future if the context makes it clear that the reference is to the future. The question that now arises is whether the interpretation can be of reference to past time where there is an overt indicator of past time, e.g. *ʕalā mulki sulaymāna* 'in Solomon's reign'. The answer is in the affirmative, as in:

Wa	ʔattabaʕū (Pfv.)		mā	tatlū (Ipfv.)	'l-	šayāṭīnu
and	they-follow		what	they-recite	the	demons
ʕalā	mulki	sulaymāna.				
in	reign	Solomon				

And they followed what the demons used to recite in Solomon's reign.

Thus the Imperfective can be used with past time reference, provided only that it also has imperfective meaning. Summarising the uses of the Imperfective and Perfective, we may say that the Perfective indicates both perfective meaning and relative past time reference, while the Imperfective indicates everything else (i.e. either imperfective meaning or relative non-past tense). The Arabic opposition Imperfective/Perfective incorporates both aspect and (relative) tense.[1]

One naturally wonders how Arabic makes finer time reference distinctions within the range covered by the Imperfective. In fact, in the absence of more specific temporal adverbials (and even usually

---

[1] The extent to which aspect or tense is predominant seems to have changed over the course of the development of Arabic. In Classical Arabic, there are examples of the Perfective with present or future time reference, for instance in wishes and curses: *laʕana-ka 'llāhu* 'may God curse you!', although the use of the Perfective with the specific marker of Future Tense, *sa-* or *sawfa* (see below), is excluded even in Classical Arabic. In modern written Arabic, overt tense markers, as discussed below, are usual, even in the presence of temporal adverbs, although it still remains true that the Perfective has perfective relative past meaning, and the Imperfective either imperfective or relative nonpast meaning. The modern vernaculars also make these finer tense distinctions, in addition to that between Perfective and Imperfective.

when they are present, especially in the modern written language), Arabic has means of indicating specifically Future Tense and Past Tense of the Imperfective (other Imperfective forms being by elimination Present). Future Tense is specified by adding *sawfa* or the prefix *sa-* before the verb, e.g. *sawfa yaktubu* or *sa-yaktubu* 'he will write'. To show the Imperfective Past, one combines the Perfective of the verb 'to be' (here functioning as an auxiliary) and the Imperfective of the main verb, e.g. *kāna yaktubu* 'he was writing, used to write'. The construction is similar to those discussed in section 1.1.2 where perfective and imperfective forms are combined to indicate both that an action is complete in itself and that it has internal structure. The Arabic form cited might equally be glossed literally as 'it happened (Pfv.) that he be writing (Ipfv.)', with a past time interpretation assigned to *yaktubu* because *kāna* has already specified the tense as Past.

In addition, Arabic has specifically Perfect forms too, formed typically with the particle *qad*. Thus an explicit Present Perfect uses the particle *qad* and the Perfective, e.g. *qad kataba* 'he has written', the Perfective being used because the verb form also has perfective and past meaning. For Past Perfect, one uses the Perfective of 'to be' and the Perfective of the main verb (i.e. 'it happened that he wrote', or rather 'it happened that he had written', since the Perfective in each case indicates relative past time), with or without *qad*: *kāna (qad) kataba* 'he had written'. For the Future Perfect, one uses the Imperfective of 'to be' with the Perfective of the main verb, again with or without *qad*: *yakūnu (qad) kataba* 'he will have written'; in fact, the Imperfective of 'to be' regularly functions as a Future Tense, since in the Present Tense Arabic has no overt copula.

An opposition similar to that of Arabic is also found in Chinese; the examples below are all from Mandarin Chinese, although a similar opposition, using different morphological material, is found in other dialects of Chinese. The opposition is between verbal forms with the suffix *-le*[1] and those lacking this suffix, e.g. for the verb *xiě* 'write',

---

[1] In addition to the verbal suffix *-le*, Mandarin Chinese also has a sentence particle *-le*, attached to the last word in the sentence (not necessarily the verb). The two are different both syntactically and semantically (Chao 1968: 246–7, 798–800), and in other dialects of Chinese there are two non-homophonous particles. The sentence-particle *-le* will not be discussed here. The account of the verb-suffix *-le* given here is based on Jaxontov (1957: 115–21), although the same uses are noted by Chao (1961: 246–8), who uses the term Perfective for verbs with the suffix

xiě-le and *xiě*. In many cases the use of *-le* is optional (this is unlike Arabic, where it is not in general possible to replace the Perfective by the Imperfective), but when it does occur *-le* indicates a past perfective situation, e.g. *Xiāo duìzhǎng xiě-le yi-fēn xìn* 'Commander Hsiao wrote a letter'. Strictly, this is relative rather than absolute past time reference, as can be seen most clearly in a time clause, e.g. *nǐ sǐ-le, wǒ zuò héshang* 'when you die, I shall become a monk', i.e. 'once you have died...'. In the negative, instead of the suffix *-le* we find *méi(you)* before the verb, e.g. *tā méi(you) lái* 'he didn't come'; this is another feature differentiating the verb suffix *-le* from sentence *-le*.

Where the reference is to a (relative) present or future situation, the form without *-le* is used, e.g. *tā xiě xìn* 'he writes letters', *tā míngtian xiě xìn* 'he'll write the letter tomorrow'. To express a relative past situation which is not perfective, this same form is used, with some indicator of time, e.g. *tā yuánlái xiě xìn* 'he formerly wrote letters' (*yuánlái* 'formerly').

4.5. Aspect and time reference in tenseless languages

In a number of West African languages, including Yoruba and Igbo, there are no specific markers of past versus present tense, although there are markers of aspect.[1] Thus in Yoruba, nonstative verbs have no marker if they have perfective meaning, and the marker *ń* before the verb if they have imperfective meaning.[2] Stative verbs have only imperfective meaning, and take no marker. In Igbo, the Imperfective of nonstative verbs is marked by *nà* before the verb. One might therefore expect that sentences with these various verbal forms would be ambiguous as to time reference. In fact, in the absence of any contextual indication of time reference (e.g. a temporal adverbial), the Imperfective forms (simple stative verb or *ń/nà* form of nonstative verb) are interpreted as referring to the present, while the Perfective forms (simple nonstative verb) are interpreted as referring to the past, for

---

-le. Jaxontov uses the label *prošedšee zaveršennoe*, i.e. 'past completed', rather than *prošedšee soveršennoe* ('past perfective'), the usual term in discussions of Slavonic languages, but notes explicitly that the uses of the Chinese forms with the verb-suffix *-le* are essentially the same as those of the Perfective Past in Russian.

[1] Welmers (1973: 345-7), from whom most of the examples below are taken.

[2] Some dialects of Yoruba further distinguish a Habitual with different markers, in which case the *ń* forms are more specifically Progressive.

instance: Yoruba *ó fẹ́ owó*, Igbo *ọ́ cọ̀rọ̀ é'gọ́* 'he wants money'; Yoruba *ó ń ṣiṣẹ́*, Igbo *ọ́ nà àrụ́ ọ́'rụ́* 'he is working, he works (habitually)'; Yoruba *ó wá*, Igbo *ọ́ byàrà* 'he came'. Only in the presence of an overt indication of time would the Imperfective forms be interpreted as referring to the past: Yoruba *ó ń ṣiṣẹ́ l'ánǎ*, Igbo *ọ́ nà àrụ́ ọ́'rụ́ écí* 'he was working yesterday'. Thus there is a close relationship between Imperfective Aspect and present time, and between Perfective Aspect and past time, in these languages without tense markers.[1] This is not too dissimilar from the situation in Arabic, discussed in section 4.4, where there is a set of forms incorporating both Past Tense and Perfective Aspect.

It is not unlikely that a very similar system obtained at a late stage in the prehistoric development of Indo-European, with aspect being marked overtly and time reference at best a secondary consequence of aspectual distinctions. If we neglect the future tense, which is a relatively late and language-particular development within the Indo-European languages, and also, for convenience, the Perfect, which does not enter into this particular argument, then it has often been assumed that Indo-European had three categories, the Present, Imperfect, and Aorist. Now, while the distinction between Present and Aorist and the forms of either can clearly be traced back to Proto-Indo-European, the same cannot be said of the Imperfect, for which the allegedly Indo-European formation with the augment and Present stem (e.g. Ancient Greek *éphere* 'he was carrying, he used to carry') is attested only in Indo-Iranian, Greek, and Hittite.[2] Latin and Balto-Slavonic have quite different formations (different also from one another), while Germanic falls outside this system by having a Past Tense undifferentiated for aspect. Thus it seems that Proto-Indo-European lacked the Imperfect, i.e. a special form combining imperfective aspect and past time reference. In ascertaining whether the tense or the aspect distinction was earlier, one may look at the formation of the separate Imperfects in the various languages: in each of the language groups mentioned above with an Imperfect/Aorist distinction, the Imperfect is formed from the so-called

---

[1] Welmers (1973: 246–7) refers to this kind of usage as 'factative', i.e. the construction in question 'expresses the most obvious fact about the verb in question, which in the case of active [i.e. nonstative—B.C.] verbs is that the action was observed or took place, but for stative verbs [and Imperfective nonstative verbs—B.C.] is that the situation obtains at present'.

[2] Kuryłowicz (1964: 134).

Present stem (not the Aorist stem), with some other indicator of Past Tense (e.g. the augment *e-*); whence the characterisation of the Imperfect as the 'Present in the Past'. The nature of the Imperfect, both synchronically and diachronically, becomes clearer if one thinks not of Present stem versus Aorist stem, but of Imperfective stem versus Perfective stem: the Perfective stem is, in isolation, usually interpreted as referring to the past (whence the Aorist); the Imperfective stem in isolation is usually interpreted as referring to the present, and to specify the combination of imperfective and past time meaning some additional marker is needed, such as the various additions to the Imperfective stem that are found in the individual languages to mark the Imperfect.

4.6. Aspect and voice

In many languages, in particular in many Indo-European languages, there are interrelations between aspect and voice (active versus passive). Since these relations are less fully discussed in the literature on aspect than are relations between aspect and tense, some space will be devoted to them here.

In a number of languages, overt expression of perfect meaning is possible only in the passive voice, and not in the active. In Russian, for instance, a sentence like *kon'jak vypit* means explicitly 'the brandy has been drunk', and not 'the brandy was drunk', which would be *kon'jak byl vypit*; but this distinction cannot be made in the active voice, where *on vypil kon'jak* corresponds to both 'he drank the brandy' and 'he has drunk the brandy'. The distinction is thus maintained only in the passive, or rather certain tenses of the passive.[1] A similar situation obtains in Irish, where the Simple Past, rather like the Russian Perfective Past, can have either perfect or nonperfect force: *an bhfacaís fós é?* 'have you seen him yet?', *an bhfacaís an páipéar inné?* 'did you see the paper yesterday?', with the verb form *facaís* (mutated to *bhfacaís* after *an*) in both examples. However, there is also a specifically Perfect form, using the Past Participle Passive, just as in Russian: *tá an dinnéar ite ag Tomás* 'Tom has eaten dinner' (literally 'dinner is having-been-eaten (*ite*) by Tom'). Once again, a distinct perfect can be maintained only in the passive. The only difference between Russian and Irish here seems to be the greater tendency in Irish to give overt expression to this perfect meaning by using the passive construction, whereas Russian

---

[1] For further discussion of the Russian Passive, including its interaction with aspect, see Harrison (1967).

has a greater tendency to neutralise the semantic distinction by using the active Perfective Past.

One of the disadvantages of this particular relationship between aspect and voice is that the perfect can be maintained as an overtly distinct category only with verbs that have a passive, i.e., for the majority of Indo-European languages, transitive verbs. This system may be compared with the slightly different relation between aspect and voice found, for instance, in the Indo-Iranian languages. Although Indo-Iranian inherited from Indo-European a three-way distinction among the simple past tenses, between Imperfect, Aorist, and Perfect, there is a tendency from the earliest period for new compound tenses to arise based on the Past Participle Passive, especially in the Perfect, on the basis of passive constructions like Sanskrit *tenedam uktam* (i.e. *tena* 'by him' *idam* 'this (neuter)' *uktam* 'said (Past Participle Passive, neuter)') 'this was said by him'. The important difference vis-à-vis Slavonic or Irish is that in Indo-Iranian the Past Passive Participle can also be formed from intransitive verbs, and has active meaning, so that corresponding in aspect (though not in voice) to *tenedam uktam* we have also in Sanskrit *sa mṛtaḥ* 'he has died'. The system is still not fully in equilibrium, because in order to express Perfect Aspect in this way, one must in the one case use an active construction (with intransitive verbs), in the other a passive construction (with transitive verbs). In the later development of this construction in Indo-Iranian there are two main changes. The one is the spread of this, originally periphrastic Perfect, construction so that it becomes the basic past tense construction: in most modern Indo-Iranian languages there is no trace of the Indo-European simple past tenses, but only descendants of originally periphrastic constructions with the Past Participle. The other change is the reanalysis of the Sanskrit-type passive *tenedam uktam* as an active, i.e. what was originally the subject of a passive construction is reinterpreted as direct object of an active construction, and the earlier passive agent is reinterpreted as subject of an active construction. This gives rise to the kind of construction known as the ergative, in which the morphological marking of the subject of a transitive verb differs from that of an intransitive verb, the latter being the same as the direct object of a transitive verb, and where moreover the verb often agrees with the direct object rather than with the subject, e.g. Hindi *aurat calī hai* 'the woman has gone' (literally 'woman (nominative) gone (feminine) is'), but *laṛke ne kitāb likhī hai* 'the boy has written a book' (literally 'boy ergative book (nominative) written (feminine)[1] is'). The final step is for even this trace of the original passive construction to be lost, so that derivatives of the original periphrastic Perfect Passive take their subject in the nominative and direct object in the accusative, there being no ergative construction; this stage is exemplified by Modern Persian: *zan raft* 'the woman went' (literally 'woman (nominative) went'), *pesar ketāb rā xarid* 'the boy bought the book' (literally 'boy (nominative) book accusative bought').

One naturally goes on to ask why this particular relation between perfect aspect and passive voice is found.[2] The perfect relates a past action to a present state, i.e. can express a present state as being the result of some past action. The older forms of the passive in many languages are likewise stative.[3] When an action involving an agent and an object takes place, the resultant change in state is usually more apparent in the object than in the agent, as in *the enemy has destroyed the city*. With transitive verbs, therefore, the most usual state resulting from an action will be the changed state of the semantic object of the action, in the example given a change in the state of the city. The perfect passive is precisely that form which predicates a change of state to the object of an action. With intransitive verbs, the change of state is apparent in the agent, so the active voice is appropriate: *John has arrived*.

[1] In Hindi, *kitāb* 'book' is feminine.

[2] The explanation given here is based on the discussion in Kuryłowicz (1964: 56–89). Although the present discussion is limited to periphrastic forms using the Indo-European Past Participle and their derivatives, Kuryłowicz notes essentially the same phenomenon with regard to the Indo-European Perfect, typically active with intransitive verbs but passive with transitive verbs at an earlier period.

[3] For instance, the German construction *das Haus ist gebaut* 'the house is (i.e. has been) built' is older than *das Haus wird gebaut* 'the house is being built'; further examples are given by Kuryłowicz (1964: 56–89).

5

Formal expression of aspectual oppositions

5.1. Morphology of aspect

5.1.0. It is not the aim of the present chapter to look in detail at the morphology of any one language or group of languages, since morphological information of this kind can readily be obtained from grammars of the individual languages, and is not in itself of interest to the study of the functioning of aspect within language systems as a whole. Rather, the aim of the present chapter is to look at recurring features, both morphological and syntactic, in the formal expression of aspectual oppositions, and especially features that recur in languages that are not related to one another and are widely separated geographically from one another; it will also be our aim to look at those features of aspectual morphology within individual languages that seem to have some bearing on the semantic functioning of the aspectual systems of these languages.

The first major division that can be made in ways of formally expressing aspectual oppositions in languages is between morphological (synthetic) and syntactic (analytic) means. Although there may be individual cases where it is difficult to decide whether a given formation is primarily morphological or syntactic, in the vast majority of cases the distinction can be drawn, and this forms a useful starting-point for our classification. A clear example of syntactic expression of aspect is in the Progressive Aspect of Yoruba, of the type *ó ń ṣiṣẹ́* 'he is working', literally 'he in work', where the verbal construction is like that of an adverbial phrase.[1] Similarly, the Progressive in English would fall under this heading, as in *I am working*, with the construction Copula verb + Predicate; even clearer is the French Progressive paraphrase *je suis en train de travailler*, literally 'I am in (the) process of working'. We shall

---

[1] Welmers (1973: 344–6).

return to syntactic expressions of aspectual oppositions later in this chapter.

Among languages that do have morphological means of expressing aspectual oppositions, we may make a distinction between those languages where there is a clearly identifiable marker of aspect (or of one member of an aspectual opposition), the forms of the verb being otherwise the same for both aspects, and those languages where this is not so. Clear examples of the former type are languages with an invariable affix indicating aspect, such as Chinese -*zhe* (Progressive) and Persian *mi-* (Imperfective). Prefixation as a marker of Perfective Aspect in Slavonic and Baltic languages, and also in Georgian, is a similar process, though slightly less systematic, in that the choice of prefix is often lexically determined (e.g. the Perfective of Russian *čitat'* 'read' is *pro-čitat'*, whereas the Perfective of *pisat'* 'write' is *na-pisat'*), and may also modify the meaning of the verb in accordance with the meaning of the prefix elsewhere in derivational morphology; in Slavonic and, to a lesser extent, in Baltic (but not in Georgian) there also exists a derivational process of imperfectivisation, whereby Imperfective verbs can be derived by suffixation from prefixed Perfectives (cp. section 5.1.1).

5.1.1. *Prefixing in Balto-Slavonic, Georgian, and Hungarian*

In view of the importance of the Slavonic aspectual system in discussions of aspect in general linguistics, it is perhaps worth spending some time in looking at the morphology of this system, both as it functions in the modern languages (especially Russian),[1] and historically.[2] From the viewpoint of the genesis of the aspectual system, a diachronic comparison may be made with the Baltic languages, and a typological comparison may be made with Georgian.

The Slavonic languages, like the older Indo-European languages generally, had originally a perfective/imperfective distinction in the Past Tense, in the Aorist/Imperfect opposition, although these forms have been lost in the majority of the modern Slavonic languages (with the exception of Bulgarian, Macedonian, and some forms of Serbo-Croatian and Sorbian). The current distinction between the Perfective and Imperfective, not restricted to Past Tense, is however a Slavonic

---

[1] For a fuller discussion, see Isačenko (1962: 350–81).

[2] A recent brief discussion is Forsyth (1972), with references to fuller discussions.

innovation, shared partly with the closely related Baltic languages, and without any systematic parallel in the other branches of Indo-European. In the modern languages Perfectives are formed from Imperfectives primarily by prefixing, less commonly by suffixing. The vast majority of prefixes used for this purpose have their origin in prepositions and/or adverbs, and as such are similar in origin to such particles as *up* in English *drink up* (cp. *drink*), or the German prefix *auf-* in *auftrinken* 'drink up' (cp. *trinken* 'drink'), or the Latin prefix *con-* in *conficere* 'complete' (cp. *facere* 'do, make'), although in these languages, in contrast to Slavonic, there is no systematic opposition of Perfective and Imperfective.

At an early stage in the development of the Slavonic languages, it is probable that prefixing a simple verb did not in itself lead to perfectivisation, and Modern Russian still contains a number of prefixed simple verbs without perfective meaning, often borrowed from Old Church Slavonic, the earliest attested Slavonic language, e.g. *pred-videt'* 'foresee', *so-stojat'* 'consist'. Subsequently, certain prefixal usages came to be interpreted as specifically perfective, although the opposition Perfective/Imperfective was certainly not yet a fully developed system offering two aspectual forms for all (or nearly all) verbs, so that those verbs that did not have specifically prefixed forms had no specifically Perfective forms. In some such cases of prefixation, the difference in meaning was purely aspectual (especially with *po-*, the most neutral prefix semantically); elsewhere, the addition of the prefix, in addition to changing the aspect of the verb, also changed its meaning, as in the relation between *rezat'* 'cut' and *ot-rezat'* 'cut-off', *raz-rezat'* 'cut-up', etc. For certain verbs where, in the modern language, the prefix is simply aspectual, it is possible that at an earlier period there was also a semantic difference, or at least that the prefix, though semantically non-empty, simply reiterated some inherent semantic feature of the verb, as with *na-pisat'* 'write' (i.e. 'write on'), *pro-čitat'* 'read' (i.e. 'read through'). Only where the prefix adds nothing to the meaning of the Imperfective verb other than perfective meaning do we have strict aspectual pairs.[1] At this stage, then, we have basically simple unprefixed verbs, which are neutral as to aspect, but may be strictly interpreted as Imperfective when they are in

---

[1] In current discussions of Russian aspect, there is much controversy over just how many such aspectual pairs, with semantically empty prefixes, there are, and a particularly negative attitude is taken by Isačenko (1962: 358–63, and passim); for discussion, see Forsyth (1970: 36–43).

Table 2. *Development of prefixed Perfective and suffixed Imperfective in Russian*

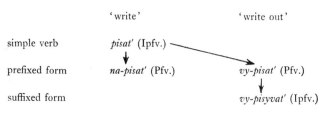

	'write'	'write out'
simple verb	*pisat'* (Ipfv.)	
prefixed form	*na-pisat'* (Pfv.)	*vy-pisat'* (Pfv.)
suffixed form		*vy-pisyvat'* (Ipfv.)

opposition to a Perfective,[1] and prefixed verbs which are for the most part Perfective; some Imperfective verbs will not have a semantically equivalent Perfective, since they may not be used with any prefix that does not affect the lexical meaning of the verb, while many Perfective verbs (all of those that are formed with meaning-changing prefixes) have no specific Imperfective counterpart.

The next stage in the systematisation of the aspectual opposition was the development of Imperfective equivalents specific to those Perfectives with semantically non-empty prefixes, and this was achieved by means of suffixal derivatives of the prefixed Perfectives; these have purely aspectual value. Examples are Old Church Slavonic *iz-bavl-j-ati* (for **iz-bav-jati*), the Imperfective of *iz-bav-iti* 'save', and Russian *ot-rez-yv-at'* 'cut off', the Imperfective of *ot-rez-at'* mentioned above. Diagrammatically, the development of the aspectual system can be represented as in table 2, where the forms lower down the page are those that developed later in the history of the formation of aspectual pairs.

In Modern Russian, then, Perfective/Imperfective pairs are related primarily either by the Perfective being a prefixed derivative of the Imperfective, or by the Imperfective being a suffixal derivative of the Perfective, the latter more particularly where the verb has a semantically non-empty prefix.

If we look at the other languages mentioned above, we find aspectual systems that are very like that of Slavonic as it was at an earlier period. Thus in the Germanic languages there are some prefixed verbs that can have perfective meaning, but there is no systematic pairing of forms with perfective and imperfective meaning, and in general no way of deriving forms with imperfective meaning from verbs with perfective meaning.[2]

---

[1] For elaboration of this point, see chapter 6 on markedness.

[2] It is possible that the prefix *ga-*, as in Gothic, originally denoted, or came to denote in some Germanic languages perfective meaning, but outside

In Lithuanian,[1] we find a situation very similar to the earlier Slavonic position: prefixing a simple verb may make it Perfective, particularly if there is otherwise no semantic change involved. Where the prefix does involve some other semantic change, Dambriūnas suggests that the verb may be either Perfective or Imperfective, or both, according to various largely idiosyncratic features, though including tense. There is a procedure for deriving specifically Imperfective forms from prefixed Perfectives, with the suffix *-inė*, but this is not as productive as the Slavonic imperfectivising suffixes. As a result, although there are several purely aspectual Perfective/Imperfective pairs in Lithuanian, their number is much smaller than in Slavonic, and the strictly aspectual system is not so well developed as in Slavonic. Latvian appears to be similar to Lithuanian, though with differences in the morphological processes used: in particular, Latvian has no imperfectivising suffix. The addition of a prefix to a simple verb may either just change the meaning, or change the meaning and add Perfective Aspect, or simply add Perfective Aspect. The pair *lasīt* (Ipfv.) – *iz-lasīt* (Pfv.) 'read' seems to be a pure aspectual pair, while *iet* 'go' and *ie-iet* 'go in' involve change of both meaning and aspect (though *ie-iet* can apparently also be used as an Imperfective). Latvian does have one (not fully productive) means of forming an Imperfective equivalent to a given prefixed Perfective, namely by using instead of the prefix the equivalent adverb. Thus corresponding to the prefix *ie-* is the adverb *iekšā* 'in(side)', so that alongside Perfective *ie-iet* there is also Imperfective *iet iekšā*. Since one can also use, as a Perfective, *ie-iet iekšā*, with double specification of the direction of motion (prefix *ie-* and adverb *iekšā*), perhaps it would be more correct to say that the real opposition is between prefixed Perfective and nonprefixed Imperfective: if one wants to indicate direction of motion, then one can use a locative adverb, though obviously there is less need to do so if the verb already has a locative prefix.

In the Baltic languages, it is not always the case that prefixing of a simple verb leads to Perfective Aspect, as it does in the Slavonic languages (excepting loans in the modern Slavonic languages from Old Church Slavonic, or calques on verbs from non-Slavonic languages), nor is there in general any way of forming Imperfectives from prefixed

---

of Gothic there is little direct evidence of such a situation, and in Modern German, for instance, *ge-* is simply a regular marker for the Past Participle, with no other meaning of its own.

[1] For the data, see Dambriūnas (1959).

Perfectives. The formation of the Perfective in Georgian is similar to that of Baltic in that there is no way of forming Imperfectives from Perfectives, although it is generally true that prefixing a simple verb makes it Perfective.[1] Georgian has a long literary tradition dating back to the fifth century, and it is possible in Georgian to trace a development similar in many ways to that in the Balto-Slavonic languages. Whether there is any direct influence of Slavonic on Georgian at an early period remains an open question; there is little direct evidence pointing to any such relationship. In Old Georgian simple verbs could be prefixed, but such prefixed verbs were not specifically Perfective. In the modern language, many loans from the older literary language still retain this latter trait, e.g. *še-icavs* 'it contains' (*še-* 'in(to)'), *gan-martavs* 'he explains' (*ga(n)-* 'out of'), and in addition certain intransitive verbs, in particular verbs of motion, do not change aspect when prefixed. For the vast majority of Modern Georgian verbs, however, the addition of a prefix makes the resultant verb Perfective (and in particular means that the resultant verb has a Future Tense, but no Present). Some prefixes simply change the aspect of a simple verb, as in *da-çer* 'write' (Imperfective *çer*) and *ga-aķeteb* 'do, make' (Imperfective *aķeteb*). In many cases, however, the prefix changes not only the aspect, but also the meaning, as with *ča-çer* 'inscribe', *gada-çer* 'copy', *gamo-içer* 'subscribe', from *çer* 'write', and *še-aķeteb* 'repair', *mo-aķeteb* 'cure', *gada-aķeteb* 'remake', from *aķeteb* 'do, make'. The question therefore arises: how does one use one of these verbs in the Imperfective, for instance as a Present? The answer is that one cannot. Either one has to use some circumlocution with the simple verb (and, for instance, an adverbial that expresses the same meaning as the prefix would; since with some verbs the prefixes have idiosyncratic meanings, this is by no means always possible), or one just uses the simple unprefixed verb, which in Georgian is, at least potentially, the Imperfective of *all* its prefixed Perfectives. Thus corresponding to the Perfective *gamo-içer* 'subscribe'[2] the Imperfective is simply *içer*, although the latter could also be taken in its simpler sense 'write for one's own benefit': *čemi bavšebisatvis me sxva žurnals viçer* 'for my children I subscribe (*v-* is the first person prefix of the verb) to another magazine'. Since the

[1] Vogt (1971: 183–6).

[2] In this form, the prefix *i-* is not a derivational prefix, but is a marker of so-called version (Vogt 1971: 118–27), and indicates something like 'for one's own sake', though in *gamoiçer* it is an obligatory part of the verb.

prefix can sometimes quite radically change the meaning of the simple verb, the possibility of interpreting a given unprefixed Imperfective may in practice be more restricted. Thus there are two Perfective verbs *še-iaraɣeba* 'arm' and *gan-iaraɣeba* 'disarm', so that in principle the Imperfective (which in this case has an aspectually empty causative prefix) *aiaraɣeb* should be ambiguous, though in practice it will usually be interpreted as 'arm', i.e. the semantically more neutral member of the set.[1] Thus although Georgian has developed a rather clear opposition between Perfective and Imperfective, the aspectual system has not developed to the extent of having an overall system of lexically equivalent aspectual pairs.

The aspectual significance of verbal prefixes in Hungarian is even less well developed than in Georgian or Baltic. The Hungarian verbal prefixes can in certain syntactic constructions be separated from their verb, rather as in German (though the precise rules determining how and when prefixes are to be separated are different in the two languages), and most of the prefixes are similar to, and easily shown to derive etymologically from, adverbs and/or postpositions (most postpositions are adverbial in origin anyway).[2] The use of these prefixes as perfectivisers comes midway between the use of prefixes or particles in German or English (*drink up*, *auftrinken*) and in Georgian or Baltic. Hungarian has no way of deriving Imperfectives from Perfectives, as in Slavonic and to some extent Lithuanian. There is one prefix, *meg-*, which has no lexical significance of its own, and is often used purely as a perfectivising prefix, as in *ír* 'write', *meg-ír* (Pfv.); although with some verbs *meg-* does have other functions, and may simply differentiate lexical items, as in *olvas* 'read' versus *meg-olvas* 'count'. Other prefixes are also sometimes used with purely aspectual meaning with certain verbs; a purely aspectual pair with the prefix *el-* (literally 'away from') would be *pusztít* 'destroy', Perfective *el-pusztít*. With most prefixes, however, which also change the meaning other than aspectually, aspectual significance is at best secondary.

The languages examined that have prefixes or verbal particles with, at least sometimes, aspectual (perfective) significance, can be arranged along the following scale according to the extent to which they have a

[1] Vogt (1971: 185) notes that authorities differ on whether they admit the meaning 'disarm' at all for the Imperfective verb.
[2] Details of the aspectual significance of Hungarian prefixes are given by Majtinskaja (1959: 173–93, especially 177–8).

fully developed system of oppositions between Perfective and Imperfective, starting with those languages with the least fully developed system: English and German, Hungarian, Baltic, Georgian, Slavonic. The relative positions of Baltic and Georgian are perhaps debatable, since they possess and lack different sets of aspectual criteria. The criteria that go most towards making a systematic set of aspectual oppositions are: the presence of an otherwise semantically empty perfectivising prefix (such as Gothic *ga-*, Hungarian *meg-*, Georgian *da-*, Lithuanian *pa-*, Slavonic *po-*, or other prefixes with more restricted sets of verbs); the possibility of forming Imperfectives from verbs where the prefix changes meaning other than just aspect (Slavonic, to some extent Lithuanian); correlations of aspectual differences with tense differences (Slavonic, Georgian, to some extent Hungarian; see section 4.1), though this is by no means a necessary factor (it does not hold for South Slavonic); and of course, the possibility of forming Perfective/ Imperfective pairs for as many verbs as possible (preferably wherever the aspectual opposition is compatible with the lexical meaning of the verb; Slavonic approaches this situation). This same arrangement of languages can also give some insight into the way in which these prefixal formations developed aspectual meaning: the addition of a prefix to a simple verb normally results in a restriction of the meaning of that verb, and one way in which such a restriction can be interpreted is as a restriction to a single unified complete action; this is by no means a necessary restriction, as is shown by those languages where verbal prefixes do not normally have aspectual significance, though particularly in the presence of semantically neutral aspectual prefixes and of processes of imperfectivisation, this can lead to the development of an aspectual system relying primarily on prefixation as a means of perfectivisation.

5.1.2. *Combined tense/aspect morphology*

In the languages whose morphology we have examined so far, the forms for the individual tenses, moods, persons, and numbers, etc., have been the same for all aspects, i.e. the only difference has been the aspect marker as such, either trivially so, as in Chinese where there are no verbal markers of tense, person, etc., or more interestingly so in languages with complex verbal morphologies like the Balto-Slavonic languages and Georgian. In such languages, aspect is clearly distinct as a morphological category from the other morphological categories expressed in the verb. Other languages present a rather different

Table 3. *Verbal morphology (Indicative Mood) of written Arabic* (kataba '*he wrote*')

		Perfective	Imperfective
Singular	3 masc.	kataba	yaktubu
	fem.	katabat	taktubu
	2 masc.	katabta	taktubu
	fem.	katabti	taktubīna
	I	katabtu	ʔaktubu
Dual	3 masc.	katabā	yaktubāni
	fem.	katabatā	taktubāni
	2	katabtumā	taktubāni
Plural	3 masc.	katabū	yaktubūna
	fem.	katabna	yaktubna
	2 masc.	katabtum	taktubūna
	fem.	katabtunna	taktubna
	I	katabnā	naktubu

picture: thus in Arabic, for instance, although there are distinct stems for the Perfective and Imperfective (e.g. respectively *katab-* and *-(a)ktub-* 'write'), the verbal endings indicating person (first, second, third), number (singular, dual, plural), and gender (masculine, feminine) are quite distinct for the two aspects. In the paradigm of the Arabic regular verb (table 3), although there are some recurrent similarities between the inflections of Perfective and Imperfective (e.g., apart from the first person singular, the suffix *-t* of the Perfective corresponds to the prefix *t-* of the Imperfective), in general there is no simple correspondence between the affixes used for the same person/gender/number in the two aspects. In the first conjugation in French, the most productive conjugation in the language, there is even less clear-cut distinction between the morphological exponency of aspect (here, the difference between Past Definite and Imperfect) and of other verbal categories; whether we look at the written or the spoken language, the stem is the same for both aspectual forms (*aim-* [ɛm]), while there is little parallelism between equivalent morphological forms of the two aspects (table 4).

The historical development of verbal morphology from Ancient to Modern Greek is interesting in this respect (table 5). In Ancient Greek, the Aorist and Imperfect have distinct stems (e.g. *graps-* (for **graf-s-*) versus *graf-* 'write'),[1] while in the majority of verbs they also have

---

[1] The initial *e-* (augment) of the finite Past Tense, which is lost if un-stressed in Modern Greek, is not relevant to the present discussion.

95

Table 4. *Past Definite and Imperfect in French* (aimer '*to love*')

		Past Definite		Imperfect	
Singular	1	j'aimai	[ɛme]	j'aimais	[ɛmɛ]
	2	tu aimas	[ɛma]	tu aimais	[ɛmɛ]
	3	il aima	[ɛma]	il aimait	[ɛmɛ]
Plural	1	nous aimâmes	[ɛmɑːm]	nous aimions	[ɛmjɔ̃]
	2	vous aimâtes	[ɛmɑːt]	vous aimiez	[ɛmje]
	3	ils aimèrent	[ɛmɛːr]	ils aimaient	[ɛmɛ]

Table 5. *Verbal morphology* (*Indicative Mood*) *in Ancient and Modern Greek* (gráfō '*I write*')

Ancient Greek

		Present	Future	Imperfect	Aorist
Singular	1	gráfō	grápsō	égrafon	égrapsa
	2	gráfeis	grápseis	égrafes	égrapsas
	3	gráfei	grápsei	égrafe	égrapse
Plural	1	gráfomen	grápsomen	egráfomen	egrápsamen
	2	gráfete	grápsete	egráfete	egrápsate
	3	gráfousi(n)	grápsousi(n)	égrafon	égrapsan

Modern Greek

		Present		Past	
		Imperfective	Perfective	Imperfective	Perfective
Singular	1	gráfo	grápso	égrafa	égrapsa
	2	gráfis	grápsis	égrafes	égrapses
	3	gráfi	grápsi	égrafe	égrapse
Plural	1	gráfume	grápsume	gráfame	grápsame
	2	gráfete	grápsete	gráfate	grápsate
	3	gráfun(e)	grápsun(e)	égrafan	égrapsan
				gráfane	grápsane

distinct endings, although in some forms there is clear parallelism between the person and number endings. The Present and Future have the same endings; the stem of the Present is the same as that of the Imperfect, while the stem of the Future is often (not always) the same as that of the Aorist (cp. section 4.1). In Modern Greek, the morphological expression of aspect has been increasingly made distinct from that of other verbal categories, so that in the modern language the only difference between equivalent forms of different aspect is the difference between the Imperfective and Perfective forms of the stem. By comparing the Ancient and Modern Greek forms in table 5, it will be seen that the endings of the Modern Greek Past Tense represent a compromise between those of the Ancient Greek Imperfect and Aorist, while the difference between the current Imperfective and Perfective stems derives historically from the difference between the Present and Aorist stems in Ancient Greek. In the non-Past Tenses, the tense distinction between Present and Future forms has been lost, being replaced by a purely aspectual distinction (the Modern Greek Future is a periphrastic formation, Imperfective *tha gráfo*, Perfective *tha grápso*).[1] In Ancient Greek, as noted above, for some verbs Future and Aorist stems differ (e.g. Present *leípō* 'I leave', Future *leípsō* 'I shall leave', but Aorist *élipon* 'I left', the last being one of the few Ancient Greek Aorists to have the same endings as a regular Imperfect); in Modern Greek there are no such discrepancies between the stem forms of Present Perfective and Past Perfective (*lípo* 'I miss', *tha lípo* 'I shall be missing', *tha lípso* 'I shall miss', *élipa* 'I was missing, used to miss', *élipsa* 'I missed'). Two final points should be made about the morphology of aspect in Modern Greek. Firstly, grammars of Modern Greek, under the influence of grammars of the ancient language, often retain the Ancient Greek names of the various tenses/aspects, e.g. Aorist rather than Perfective Past, Imperfect rather than Imperfective Past; though where there are no equivalent aspectual forms in the ancient language then a terminology corresponding more to the system of the modern language is used (e.g. for the Perfective and Imperfective Future). Secondly, the rigid separation of aspectual from other morphological categories is true only of the Active Voice; in the Passive (Medio-passive), the differences between Aorist and Imperfect, and between Present and Future, were much greater in Ancient Greek than in the Active Voice, and even in Modern Greek these differences have not been levelled out, at least not to the same consistent extent as in the Active Voice.

The fusion of the morphological markers of aspect and other categories in such forms as the Aorist and Imperfect of the Indo-European languages, together with the restriction of this particular aspectual opposition, in most cases, to the past tense, may explain why forms which are differentiated aspectually, such as the Aorist and Imperfect, are traditionally referred to as tenses, rather than aspectual forms of the same tense.[2] In Russian, the Perfective and Imperfective Past have the same endings, so that it is relatively straightforward to separate the

---

[1] If the Ancient Greek Future does derive from a form which was originally aspectual, then this morphological form has gone full circle from aspectual to temporal to aspectual again.

[2] It should be noted, however, that a small number of Slavists, in particular, insist that the difference between Aorist and Imperfect in Indo-European

element (prefix or suffix) that marks aspect from the morphological markers of tense or person and number. In Ancient Greek one can isolate a marker of the Aorist/Imperfect distinction (typically the -*s* suffix in the Aorist), but the person and number endings are still different as between Aorist and Imperfect; in French one cannot even regularly isolate a morphological segment corresponding to the aspectual distinction between Past Definite and Imperfect. Thus the morphology of languages like Ancient Greek and French does not provide so overt a marker of aspect as in languages like Russian. In languages that do have a morphological distinction between the aspectual stems (whether or not the verbal inflections are otherwise the same for all aspects), the precise way in which the distinction is made morphologically depends on the overall morphological structure of the given language, and falls strictly within the province of morphology, rather than the general theory of aspect. Thus we find (with imperfective forms first): affixation (Russian *čitat' – pro-čitat'* 'read', Ancient Greek *élūon – élūsa* 'I loosed'), internal change (Ancient Greek *éleipon – élipon* 'I left', Arabic *kataba – yaktubu* 'he wrote/is writing'), suppletion (Russian *brat' – vzjat'* 'take', Georgian *xedav – naxav* 'see', Ancient Greek *esthíō* 'I eat' – *éfagon* 'I ate', Modern Greek *léo – pó* 'I say'), lack of differentiation (Russian *ženit'* 'marry', Georgian *čam* 'eat'), just as elsewhere in the morphologies of the languages concerned.

5.2. Syntactic expressions of aspectual oppositions

5.2.1. *Locative expressions of aspectual oppositions*

5.2.1.1. Progressive and imperfective aspect

In many languages, belonging to various genetic and geographical groupings, there is similarity between the formal expression of imperfective aspect, especially progressive aspect, and various locative adverbial phrases.

The most widespread parallel is between progressive aspect and expressions referring to the place where something is located, though in some languages, as noted below, this locative form of the verb is also used with habitual meaning, i.e. is imperfective rather than just progressive. The basic characteristic of this form of expression is that, in

and other languages is one of tense, not of aspect; see, for instance, Havránek (1939).

order to say 'he is working', a paraphrase of the type 'he is in/at work-(ing)' is used. The Modern English expression *he is working* does not show any trace, synchronically, of being a locative construction, although there are overtly locative paraphrases, like *he is at work, at prayer.* However, in older stages of the English language one form of the Progressive was overtly locative, with a verbal noun preceded by a locative preposition, most typically *at*, though also *in*, *on*, or the alternant *a'*, as in archaic and dialectal *Fred's been a-singing.* Some of the related Germanic languages have similar locative possibilities for the expression of progressive meaning, though usually as a highly marked form, i.e. only where it is necessary overtly to indicate progressive meaning, as in Dutch *hij is aan het tuinieren* 'he is gardening', literally 'he is at/on the gardening', with the verbal noun in *-en*. Icelandic has a more regular Progressive construction using *vera að* plus the Infinitive, i.e. the verb 'to be' plus a preposition whose basic meaning is 'in, at', also 'to', e.g. *jeg er að lesa* 'I am reading'.

An even fuller expression of progressive meaning in English, though not a particularly natural one in most circumstances, would be a locative expression containing the noun *process*, e.g. *he is in the process of getting up.* In some languages, progressive meaning can regularly be expressed by using a noun having the same meaning as English *process*; thus in French, if it is necessary to indicate progressive meaning overtly, this can be done by using the construction *être en train de* 'to be in the process of', e.g. *je suis en train d'écrire une lettre* 'I am (in the process of) writing a letter'.

Perhaps the most widespread use of locative expressions for progressive aspect in Indo-European is in the Celtic languages, although it should be noted that here it is the exception, rather than the rule, for such expressions to be explicitly progressive, rather than covering the whole imperfective; in Irish, the forms are specifically progressive. In Irish, Scots Gaelic, and Welsh, the basic construction is the same: the verb 'to be' is used with a locative preposition and the verbal noun of the verb in question, and in Irish and written Scots Gaelic the nominal nature of the verb in this construction is shown by putting the direct object in the genitive, rather than the accusative (similarly, pronoun direct objects in all three languages occur as possessive pronouns). In Welsh, the preposition used is *yn* (usually *'n* after a vowel), e.g. *y mae hi'n gweithio* 'she is working', literally 'is she in work(ing)',[1] *y mae hi'n ein taro ni* 'she is hitting us', literally 'is she in our hitting us'. However,

---

[1] In the Celtic languages, the verb regularly precedes the subject.

Formal expression of aspectual oppositions

this form can also be used with stative verbs and with habitual meaning: *y mae hi'n hoffi coffi* 'she likes coffee', *y mae hi'n gweithio bob dydd* 'she works every day'. In Irish and Scots Gaelic the preposition used is *ag* (with alternant *a'* in Scots Gaelic) 'at'; in Irish this Progressive contrasts with a non-Progressive Present, while in Scots Gaelic the original Progressive form has replaced the other verbal forms, apart from those with perfective meaning, i.e. has become an Imperfective. Characteristic examples from Irish are: *tá sé ag teacht* 'he is coming', *tá sé ag dúnadh an dorais* 'he is closing the door' (where *dorais* is the genitive of *doras* 'door', cp. *dúnann sé an doras* 'he closes the door'); from Scots Gaelic: *tha e a' seinn* 'he is singing, he sings', *tha e 'gam bhualadh* 'he is hitting' hits me' (the preposition *ag* with the possessive pronoun *mo* 'my' is realised as *'gam*). In Irish and Scots Gaelic, there are rather different constructions used with the verbal nouns of some stative verbs, as discussed in section 5.2.1.2.

Although the parallelism between progressive and locative constructions in the Celtic languages is very close, it is not absolute; there are differences of detail between the two constructions. In Welsh, for instance, although the preposition *yn* 'in' takes the nasal mutation,[1] the *yn* of the periphrastic verbal construction does not; contrast *yng Nghaerdydd* 'in Cardiff' (*Caerdydd* 'Cardiff') with *y mae hi'n canu* 'she is singing' (not **y mae hi'ng nghanu*). Moreover, the initial vowel of the preposition *yn* may not normally be elided, although it may be in the periphrastic verbal construction; thus not **y mae hi'ng Nghaerdydd* 'she is in Cardiff', but *y mae hi yng Nghaerdydd*.

In Georgian, the specifically Future forms of most verbs can only be used in the Perfective Aspect, e.g. *Soso da-çers* 'Soso will write', but not 'Soso will be writing'. However, some dialects have a periphrastic Future Progressive, with the nominal form of the verb and the postposition *-ši* 'in' with the Future of the verb 'to be', e.g. *Soso çera-ši ikneba* 'Soso will be writing', literally 'Soso writing-in will-be'. This same construction can be used in other tenses, e.g. *Soso çera-ši aris* 'Soso is writing', though here only if it is necessary to give overt expression to the progressive meaning (cp. French *être en train de*); in

[1] Mutation is a change in the initial consonant of a word when it occurs in certain environments in the sentence. There are three mutations in Welsh: soft, spirant, and nasal, in addition to the radical (unmutated) form. For instance, the preposition *i* 'to, into' requires the soft mutation: *Caerdydd* 'Cardiff', but *i Gaerdydd* 'to Cardiff'.

the Future the periphrasis is commoner, because otherwise one must sacrifice explicit mention of both Future Tense and Progressive Aspect, if one just uses the Present *Soso çers* 'Soso is writing' or 'Soso writes', which can be interpreted in the appropriate context with future meaning.[1]

In Mandarin Chinese, one way of indicating Progressive Aspect is to use the form *zài* '(be) in' before the main verb, with or without preceding *zhù* 'live, reside', *zhèng* 'just, precisely', e.g. *tā (zhèng)zài niàn shū-ne* 'he is studying'.

Locative expressions of progressive aspect are quite widespread in African languages.[2] In Yoruba, for instance, the form meaning '(be) in' is *ní* (allomorph *l'* before vowels), whilst the Progressive Aspect of verbs uses the form *ń* (allomorph *l'* before vowels), e.g. *ó ń lọ* 'he is going', literally 'he in go'. As in Welsh, there is a slight difference between the progressive and the strictly locative constructions (which latter is also used with temporal expressions, e.g *l'óní* 'today (adverb)', cp. *òní* 'today (noun)'): in Yoruba the difference between *ní* and *ń*, in Welsh between *yn* + radical and *yn* + nasal mutation. Some speakers of Yoruba use this *ń* form essentially only with progressive meaning, and have a different form (at least as a possibility) for Habitual Aspect, while other speakers use the *ń* form freely in both senses.[3] Igbo has the locative form *nà* 'in' (before vowels *n'*), e.g. *ọ́ nọ̀ nà Kánừ* 'he is in Kano', and uses the same preposition in the Imperfective of nonstative verbs (i.e. encompassing progressive meaning), e.g. *ọ́ nà àgá* 'he is going, he (habitually) goes', literally 'he in go'. Again, there are differences of detail between progressive and locative constructions, concerning deletability of the vowel of *nà*, also the fact that in Igbo the locative, unlike the progressive construction, requires a locative verb e.g. *nọ̀* 'be (at)'. In Kpelle, the usual way of indicating location is with *káa*. Etymologically, this derives from the singular imperative of the verb 'to see', but synchronically it functions solely as a locative marker,[4] e.g. *`káa ńeɣìi sû* 'it is in the pot', literally 'it (the low tone modification of *káa* to *`káa* indicates the third person subject) in pot inside'. In the progressive construction (which in Kpelle has strictly progressive meaning), one possibility is again to use this *káa*, though it may be

---

[1] Tschenkéli (1958: 83–4).

[2] For the data, see Welmers (1973: chapters 11 and 12).

[3] Rowlands (1969: 60–1).

[4] For instance, in that one could not use the Imperative plural here; cp. French *voici* and *voilà*, originally 'see here!' and 'see there!'

omitted, e.g. either *a pâi* (literally 'he come') or `*kâa pâi* (literally 'he in come') 'he is coming'. Moving further southwards, we find a similar situation in Shona. Here location is expressed by *rí* 'be (at)', which agrees with its subject like a verb, with a class-marker on the stem of the following noun, such as *ku-* 'at', e.g. *bhúkù rírí kùchìkórò* 'the book is at school'. The same construction, with *ku-*, is used for Progressive Aspect, e.g. *tìrí kùfúndá chìMànyíkà* 'we are studying ChiManyika', literally 'we-be at-study ChiManyika (a dialect of Shona)'. Thus there is ample evidence from such widely divergent language families as Indo-European and Niger-Congo for a relation between location and progressive aspect.

Although such adverbial constructions are perhaps the clearest indicators of locative expression of progressive meaning, another possibility would be the use of an auxiliary verb whose function is otherwise primarily locative, and similarly where an etymologically locative verb comes to be used as a progressive auxiliary we have diachronic evidence of such a relation. In Italian, the Progressive is formed with the verb *stare* 'stand', as in *sto cantando* 'I am singing', literally 'I-stand singing', although in this usage there is no necessary suggestion that I am literally standing, i.e. the verb of location is used simply as a marker of the Progressive Aspect. The progressive auxiliaries in Spanish (e.g. *estoy cantando* 'I am singing') and Portuguese (e.g. *estou cantando* 'I am singing') derive etymologically from the Latin verb *stare* 'stand', though in the modern Iberian languages they are used primarily in the sense 'to be (somewhere, or temporarily)'; these verbs are further discussed below (section 5.2.1.2). Similar in function and origin are Scots Gaelic *tha* 'is' and Irish *tá* (*sé*) '(he) is'. In discussing Mandarin Chinese, we noted that one way of expressing the Progressive was to use *zhùzai*, literally 'live at'. A similar construction, though perhaps rather less closely linked to its etymological origin, occurs in a number of North Indian languages, using the Perfect Participle of the verb Hindi-Urdu *rəhna*, Punjabi *rəẏna* 'live, stay, remain'. The ordinary non-Progressive forms in these languages typically already contain the Present Participle and the verb 'to be', which have ousted the simple verb forms, so that in Hindi, for instance, 'I go' is *mɜy cəlta hũ* (Punjabi *mɜy janda vã*), literally 'I going am'. In order to give overt expression to Progressive Aspect, the appropriate forms are Hindi-Urdu *mɜy cəl rəha hũ*, Punjabi *mɜy ja rẏa vã*, literally 'I go having-remained am'.

Some attention must now be given to possible reasons for this relation between locative and progressive. The clue to the relation is perhaps in English expressions like *to be in the process of doing something* or *to be in progress*, in which we see that we can refer to some instance of a process by viewing the whole of the situation as if it were spatial, when it is quite natural to refer to some specific point of the situation as being 'in' that situation. Thus really, the only requirement is that we should be able to transpose from space to time, and languages do this quite readily already in the use of originally locative prepositions, etc., as temporal, e.g. *on the table, on Friday*. English also has an expression *to be in the habit of doing something*, so that it might be tempting to account for the extension of locatives to being used with habitual meaning as an analogous process. However, this analogy seems dubious, for the following reasons. The expression *in the habit of* seems much more parochial to English than is *in the process of* (cp. French *être en train de*, but *avoir l'habitude de*, literally 'to have the habit of'). Moreover, of the languages examined where habitual meaning is expressed by means of a locative, it is always the case that progressive meaning is also expressed as a locative, indeed it is usually the case that the same locative construction is used for both meanings. Thus one can establish a certain implicational relation between locative expression of progressive and of habitual meaning: the locative expression of progressive meaning is basic, and only if a language has this possibility can it further extend the same form to habitual meaning, and this extension is rather an extension of the earlier progressive to become the only imperfective form.

5.2.1.2. Contingent state

One other area where there seems to be evidence of a link between locative and aspect concerns being in a state, rather than in the process of doing something, since here again a large number of languages use expressions that are, or derive from, locative constructions. A particularly clear set of examples is provided by certain stative verbs in Irish and Scots Gaelic, since, although these are used as verbal nouns with the verb Irish *tá*, Scots Gaelic *tha*, the precise construction used is rather different from the Progressive.[1] A literal translation of the sentence meaning 'he is sitting' would be 'is he in his sitting', where the words for 'in' and 'his' are contracted, as regularly in other constructions where they come together: Irish *tá sé ina shuí*, Scots Gaelic

---

[1] As noted above, English treats such expressions as Progressive, but many other languages do not (section 1.2.2).

tha e 'na shuidhe. Similar expressions are found with nouns other than verbal nouns denoting states, e.g. Scots Gaelic *tha e 'na shlainte* 'he is in health', literally 'is he in-his health'.

The type of state that is of particular interest for present purposes is one that is temporary, or contingent, rather than temporally unrestricted, or absolute.[1] The distinction between absolute and contingent state is made in Irish and Scots Gaelic (though there are also many idiomatic usages falling outside of the strict semantic-formal correspondence set up here) by the distinction between two verbs: the copula *is* (deriving from the Proto-Indo-European verb 'to be'), and the verb Irish *tá*, Scots Gaelic *tha* (deriving from the verb meaning 'stand'. In Irish there are thus two ways of saying 'the paper is white': *is bán an páipéar é* and *tá an páipéar bán*. However, the two differ in meaning: the former simply tells us that the paper is white, while the second implies that the whiteness of the paper is only a temporary state (e.g. it has not yet been written on). In strictly locative use, incidentally, only *tá/tha* is possible for 'be', e.g. Irish *tá mo thigh anso* 'my house is here'. The use of *tá/tha*, especially in view of its etymology, is already an instance of a locative expression for contingent state. In Scots Gaelic this is taken a stage further with noun phrase predicates: after *tha* the noun phrase predicate is constructed with the locative preposition *an* 'in', e.g. *tha e 'na fhear*, literally 'is he in-his (*'na* for *an a*) man', meaning 'he is a man', i.e. has become a man through a change of state; contrast *is fear e* 'he is a man'.[2]

The use of a verb of locative etymology, though without any difference in the adjective, to express contingent state is found in Spanish and Portuguese; the verb in question derives from Latin *stare* 'to stand'. We may take Spanish first, in which the relation between location and contingent state is particularly clear; although it should be noted that, in both languages, there is no way of marking contingent state with a

---

[1] This is the terminology of Anderson (1973: 5).

[2] In Welsh, *yn* (this time with yet a different mutation, the soft mutation) occurs with adjectival and nominal predicates, though the distinction between predicates with *yn* and those without is not that between contingent and absolute state. The difference between *y mae hi'n athrawes* (literally 'is she in teacher') and *athrawes ydy hi* (literally 'teacher is she') 'she is a teacher' is one of emphasis: the latter sentence stresses the predicate. Similarly, *y mae'r papur yn wyn* 'the paper is white' does not imply contingent state.

predicative noun, when only the copula *ser* is possible. In Spanish, for location the translation of 'to be' is *estar*, whether or not the location is temporary, as in *Madrid está en España* 'Madrid is in Spain'. With adjectives, *ser* is used for absolute state and *estar* for contingent state, thus giving a distinction between, for 'Juan is ill', *Juan es enfermo* (i.e. he is an invalid) and *Juan está enfermo* (i.e. is now ill, but can be expected to recover, or was until recently in good health). In Portuguese the same distinction exists with adjectives: *aquele camarada é enjoada* 'that fellow is boring', but: *o tempo está quente (hoje)* 'the weather is hot (today)'.[1] In Portuguese, both *ser* and *estar* may be used of location, with the same absolute/contingent distinction as for adjectives: *a casa é no Flamengo* 'the house is in Flamengo' versus *João está em casa* 'João is at home'. Given the original meaning of *estar* (Latin *stare*) as 'to stand', it is clear that Portuguese has innovated here in extending the absolute/contingent distinction to locative predicates as well: once the overt link between *estar* as an expression of contingent state and the earlier use of *estar* to indicate location is lost, *estar* comes to be felt as another form of copula alongside *ser*; Spanish, on the other hand, with its consistent use of *estar* as locative, is closer to the origin of the contingent use of *estar* in its general locative use, being in a state like being in a place.

In Russian, many expressions of contingent state, which typically involve adjectives, have paraphrases with overtly locative phrases; the glosses below are literal rather than idiomatic English.[2] Thus in near-synonymy with *general izumljen* 'the general is amazed' we have *general v izumlenii* 'the general is in amazement', cp. *general v zdanii* 'the general is in the building'. Similarly, we have sentences like *general prišel v otčajanie* 'the general came into despair', cp. *general vošel v zdanie* 'the general came into the building'. There is again a slight difference between strict motion into a place and entering a state: with the former the usual verb is *vojti*, Past Tense *vošel*, literally 'go/come in', while with the latter the verb is *prijti*, literally 'go/come to(wards), arrive'. The same pattern is found with transitive verbs: *poraženie privelo generala v otčajanie* 'the defeat brought the general into despair', cp. *ad"jutant vvel generala v zdanie* 'the aide brought the general into the building'.

---

[1] Data from Thomas (1969: 226–31).
[2] For these and similar Russian examples, see Miller (1972). Other examples of locative expressions of aspect are given in Anderson (1973).

5.2.1.3. Direction and aspect

Similar to, though apparently less common than, the use of locative expressions to indicate progressive meaning is the use of directional expressions for prospective aspectual meaning and for perfect meaning, or at least for some subset of these: motion towards serving as the model for prospective meaning, and motion from as the model for perfect meaning. Thus in English, one way of expressing prospective meaning is with *go*, e.g. *I'm going to write a letter*, cp. French *je vais écrire une lettre*. Igbo has exactly the same construction type: *ǫ̀ gà àbyá* 'he's going to come', literally 'he go come'. In some other West African languages, the verb used is 'come' rather than 'go', e.g. Fante *ɔ̀bɛ́bà* 'he's going to come', literally 'he come come', presumably in the sense of 'come to'.[1] In French, *venir de*, literally 'come from', is used to express recent perfect meaning, as in *je viens d'écrire la lettre* 'I have just written the letter', as if I were emerging from being engaged in some activity.

5.2.2. *Perfect as present plus past*

5.2.2.0. In looking at ways of expressing the Perfect in various languages, we shall be particularly interested in ways that languages use of giving overt expression to both the idea of past situation and the idea of present state, i.e. of combining the two characteristics of the meaning of the perfect in one means of expression.

One way of doing this is found in the Celtic languages, which use a construction literally translatable into English as 'I am after writing the letter' for 'I have written the letter': the verb 'to be' is in the Present Tense, while the use of the temporal preposition 'after' before the main verb clearly puts the action at a point prior in time. Thus in Welsh we have *yr ydwyf i wedi ysgrifennu'r llythyr* 'I have written the letter', literally 'am I after writing the letter'. In Scots Gaelic the preposition used is *air* 'after', e.g. *tha an t-each air briseadh cas a' bhalaich* 'the horse has broken the boy's foot', literally 'is the horse after breaking (the) foot of-the boy'. The Irish for 'after' is *tar éis*, used with the verbal noun in *táim tar éis teacht isteach*, literally 'I-am after coming in', although in Irish this form has recent perfect meaning, i.e. 'I have just (this moment) come in'.

A common way of combining present and past meaning is to use the

---

[1] Welmers (1973: 353–4).

present tense of an auxiliary verb with a past participle: the present auxiliary conveys the present meaning, while the past participle conveys that of past action. Thus we find, with the auxiliary 'to be', forms like Bulgarian *Ivan e došəl*, French *Jean est arrivé*, Italian *Gianni è arrivato*, German *Hans ist angekommen* 'John has arrived'. In Bulgarian the same construction is used with transitive verbs: *Ivan e kupil knigata* 'John has bought the book', literally 'is having-bought'. In the Romance and Germanic languages, many (in English and Spanish, for instance, all) verbs take the auxiliary 'have': *John has bought a book*, French *Jean a acheté un livre*, Italian *Gianni ha comprato un libro*, Spanish *Juan ha comprado un libro*, German *Hans hat ein Buch gekauft*.

In many modern Romance (e.g. French), Germanic (e.g. most forms of German), and Slavonic (most except Bulgarian and Macedonian) languages, these forms are not specifically perfect in meaning, but usually have taken on nonperfect meaning as well, i.e. in the modern languages there is a discrepancy between form (which includes both present and past) and meaning (which is often just past).[1] In some languages, however, this discrepancy has been lost by removing overt reference to the present. Thus in Russian, there is no possibility of using the Present Tense of the auxiliary in the (only) Past Tense, e.g. *Kolja kupil knigu* 'Kolya bought (has bought) the book', where Old Russian would have had a construction like *Kolja e kupil knigu*, with *e* 'is'; in Modern Russian, it is usual to describe forms like *kupil* as simply the Past Tense, without referring them to their etymological origins as Past Participles. However, some other Slavonic languages have not carried out this tidying-up process to the same extent, e.g. Czech *koupil jsem knihu* 'I bought the book', literally 'having-bought I-am book' (although there is no auxiliary in the third person, e.g. *koupil* 'he bought'). In Bulgarian, the auxiliary is still retained, but there is no conflict since the form still has strictly perfect meaning; see, however, section 5.2.2.1.

A consistent differentiation between Aorist without auxiliary and Perfect with auxiliary is found in some of the languages of Northern India, e.g. Hindi, Urdu, and Punjabi. Both Aorist and Perfect are formed with the Past Participle Active, and in the Perfect this is accompanied by the Present Tense of the auxiliary verb 'to be', while in the Aorist there is no auxiliary. Thus we have Hindi-Urdu *mɛ̃y bəca*

[1] A similar discrepancy is found in Latin, in the Passive, where *Caesar necatus est*, literally 'Caesar killed is', can mean either 'Caesar has been killed' or 'Caesar was killed'.

'I escaped', but *mǝy bǝca hũ* 'I have escaped', literally 'I escaped am'; and in Punjabi *ó bár gya* 'he went out', literally 'he out gone', but *ó bár gya e* 'he has gone out'.

As an example of a non-Indo-European language where the expression of the Perfect combines Present auxiliary and Past Participle, we may cite Finnish, where we find the construction type *minä olen saanut* 'I have received', literally 'I am having-received', with the Past Participle *saanut*. The simple Past Tense would be *minä sain*. In the negative, the only difference between Past and Perfect is the presence of the auxiliary in the latter, i.e. *minä en saanut* 'I did not receive', *minä en ole saanut* 'I have not received'. In Georgian too the Perfect, at least in certain forms, combines the Present Tense of the verb 'to be' with a Past Participle (see section 5.2.2.1).

By varying the tense of the auxiliary, the languages cited above that use the Present Tense of 'to be' or 'to have' in forming the Perfect can form other tenses of the Perfect, e.g. the Past Perfect (Pluperfect) and Future Perfect: Welsh *yr oeddwn i wedi ysgrifennu'r llythyr*, French *j'avais écrit la lettre*, Bulgarian *napisal bjax pismoto*, Finnish *minä olin kirjanut kirjeen* 'I had written the letter'. In those Slavonic languages where what was once the Perfect is now a simple Past Tense, there is no separate Future Perfect, and a separate Pluperfect is either rare (e.g. Czech), or obsolescent (e.g. Polish), or obsolete (e.g. Russian).

5.2.2.1. Perfect and inferential

Several languages have special inferential verb forms, to indicate that the speaker is reporting some event that he has not himself witnessed, but about whose occurrence he has learnt at second hand (though without, incidentally, necessarily casting doubt on the reliability of the information).[1] A distinct inferential occurs, for instance, in Turkish, Bulgarian, Georgian, and Estonian. To some extent this is an areal feature: thus Bulgarian has apparently developed the Inferential (absent from the other Slavonic languages and older Bulgarian) under Turkish influence, and the same could be true of Georgian; with Estonian, however, we are presumably dealing with an independent development. The point that is of particular interest in the present

---

[1] Lewis (1967: 101) uses the term 'inferential' for Turkish, i.e. the speaker infers rather than witnesses some event; in Bulgarian grammar the term *preizkazvane*, literally 'renarration' is used, although there is no necessary connection with indirect speech.

context, however, is a close formal and, it will be suggested, more than formal relation between inferential and perfect. The formal relation exists in Bulgarian, Georgian, and Estonian, in all of which the Inferential form for the Past Tense consists of a Past Participle plus the Present Tense of the verb 'to be', i.e. a form which has been shown in this chapter to be characteristic of the perfect.

The clearest example is Georgian, where the so-called Perfect is in fact both perfect and inferential in meaning, and the clearest forms to discuss are the Passive (and certain related intransitive) forms of this, e.g. *ga-v-zrd-il-var* 'I have (so it seems) been brought up, educated' or 'I have (so it seems) grown up', where *ga-* is the prefix indicating Perfective Aspect, *v-* the prefix indicating a first person subject, *zrd* the stem of the verb, *-il* the suffix of the Past Participle Passive; and *var* the same as *var* 'I am'. Literally, this form can be glossed as approximately 'I am having-been-brought-up' or 'I am having-grown-up'. The important point to note is the combination of Present Tense of the auxiliary with the Past Participle of the main verb.

In Bulgarian, the relation between Perfect and Inferential is slightly more complex. Taking firstly the non-Inferential forms, we have the Aorist (e.g. *pisax* 'I wrote', *pisa* 'he wrote'), the Imperfect (*pišex* 'I was writing', *pišeše* 'he was writing'), and the Perfect, formed with the Past Participle Active from the Aorist stem and the Present Tense of the auxiliary 'to be' (*pisal səm* 'I have written', *pisal e* 'he has written'). In the Inferential forms corresponding to these three, we normally have throughout compound formations utilising the Past Participle Active and the Present Tense of the auxiliary: thus for the Aorist *pisal səm* 'I (apparently) wrote'; for the Imperfect *pišel səm* 'I was (apparently) writing', with the Past Participle formed on the Imperfect stem; for the Perfect *pisal bil* 'I have (apparently) written' (with the Past Tense of the auxiliary), i.e. there is no formal difference between the non-Inferential Perfect and the Inferential Aorist. Actually, the situation is not quite so simple, since in the third person the non-Inferential Perfect and Inferential Aorist forms are usually kept distinct by the omission of the auxiliary in the non-Perfect forms, i.e. *pisal e* 'he has written' (non-Inferential Perfect), but *pisal* 'he (apparently) wrote' (Inferential Aorist). To this extent, then, Bulgarian has differentiated the Perfect (always with an auxiliary) from the Inferential, although elsewhere the close parallelism between the formal expression of the two categories is quite apparent.

In Estonian, although special Inferential forms exist corresponding to most non-Inferential forms (i.e. not just for Past Tenses, including the Present Perfect), it is only with the Past Tenses that a formal relation between Inferential and Perfect is found; in fact, given the rest of Estonian morphology, this is the only place where the parallelism could be expressed. The basic marker of the Inferential is the verbal suffix -*vat*. In the non-Inferential forms, the non-Perfect Past is a simple form, with the Past Tense suffix -*s*, e.g. *tema kirjanus* 'he wrote'; in the Perfect, we find the Past Participle in -*nud* with the Present Tense of the auxiliary 'to be', e.g. *tema on kirjutanud* 'he has written', cp. *tema on* 'he is'. In the corresponding Inferential forms, the overt difference between non-Perfect Past and Present Perfect is lost, instead for both there is a compound form with the Inferential of the auxiliary 'to be' and the Past Participle Active, e.g. *tema olevat kirjutanud* 'he (apparently) wrote' or 'he has (apparently) written', cp. *tema olevat* 'he is (apparently)', i.e. here the normally Perfect formation (Present auxiliary plus Past Participle) expresses inferential rather than perfect meaning.

Having noted the formal identity or near-identity in these languages between Perfect and Inferential, we must now look for an explanation for this identity. With the perfect, a past event is related to a present state, in other words the past event is not simply presented per se, but because of its relation to a present state. With the inferential, the past event is again not presented simply per se, rather it is inferred from some less direct result of the action (e.g. a second-hand report, or prima facie evidence, such as the wetness of the road leading to the inference that it has been raining, even when the raining itself has not been directly witnessed). Thus the semantic similarity (not, of course, identity) between perfect and inferential lies in the fact that both categories present an event not in itself, but via its results, and it is this similarity that finds formal expression in languages like Georgian, Bulgarian, and Estonian.[1]

---

[1] For a similar explanation, see Lytkin and Timušev (1961: 886), who discuss the Inferential in Komi, another Finno-Ugric language. Sere-brennikov (1960: 66) lists the following languages known to him where there is a close formal relation, down to identity, between the expression of perfect and inferential meaning: Turkic languages; the Uralic languages Nenets (Yurak-Samoyed), Finnish, Estonian, Mari (Cheremis), Komi (Zyryan), Udmurt (Votyak), Mańśi (Vogul); Georgian; and the Indo-European languages Latvian, Bulgarian, and Albanian. Turkic influence could account for Georgian, Bulgarian, and Albanian in this list, and Balto-Finnic influence for Latvian, but it is harder to account genetically for the similarity between the Turkic and (some) Uralic languages.

6

Markedness

6.0.   The intuition behind the notion of markedness in linguistics is that, where we have an opposition with two or more members (e.g. perfective versus imperfective), it is often the case that one member of the opposition is felt to be more usual, more normal, less specific than the other (in markedness terminology, it is unmarked, the others are marked).[1] It is clearly insufficient to rely solely on an intuitive concept of markedness, and in this chapter a number of criteria that give more content to these intuitions are presented.[2] The criteria are of varying nature (semantic, morphological, statistical), and are logically independent of one another. In many cases all criteria, or the clear majority of the criteria, point in the same direction, and here one can be reasonably certain of the appropriate assignment of markedness values. Often, however, the criteria conflict, and here one has to decide what weight must be attached to each criterion. Examples of such conflicts are cited below; in general, the morphological criteria are the least telling, since the morphology often reflects systematic correspondences of an earlier period in the history of a language.[3] It is not, at least not necessarily, the case that all oppositions will have an unmarked member and a marked member or members; in some oppositions, all members may be equally marked.[4] Finally, markedness is apparently not an all-or-none choice

---

[1] Markedness was first introduced into linguistics by the Prague School phonologists; see for instance Trubetzkoy (1939: chapter III). For a more recent discussion of markedness in phonology, see Chomsky and Halle (1968: chapter 9). Markedness was introduced into discussion of syntactic and semantic oppositions by Jakobson (1932).

[2] The choice of criteria follows in large measure the discussion in Greenberg (1966), a major recent contribution to markedness theory in linguistics, including syntax and semantics.

[3] Compare section 5.2.2.0.

[4] In phonology, such oppositions are often called equipollent, as opposed to privative oppositions.

(marked versus unmarked), since there are oppositions where the markedness difference between the members is very great, and oppositions where the difference is much less, i.e. there can be degrees of markedness. All of these possibilities are illustrated below.

6.1. Markedness and semantics

One of the most decisive criteria is that, in many cases, the meaning of the unmarked category can encompass that of its marked counterpart. The clearest example of this situation is where overt expression of the meaning of the marked category is always optional, i.e. where the unmarked category can always be used, even in a situation where the marked category would also be appropriate. Thus Italian and Spanish have Progressives very similar in meaning to that of English: Italian *sto scrivendo*, Spanish *estoy escribiendo*, English *I am writing*. However, in Spanish and Italian these forms can always, without excluding progressive meaning, be replaced by the non-Progressive forms *scrivo, escribo*, whereas in English changing *I am writing* to *I write* necessarily involves a shift to nonprogressive meaning. Compare also the following Italian example, where the Progressive and the Imperfect are used in parallel: *Il Pizzi era in cucina e stava rimestando* (Progressive) *la polenta. La moglie preparava* (Imperfect) *la tavola e il ragazzo . . . metteva* (Imperfect) *legna sul fuoco* 'Pizzi was in the kitchen and was mixing (Progressive) the polenta. His wife was laying (Imperfect) the table and the boy . . . was putting (Imperfect) wood on the fire'.[1] In such cases, we may say quite strictly that the marked category signals the presence of some feature, while the unmarked category simply says nothing about its presence or absence.[2]

The situation in the Slavonic languages is rather similar, though not identical. The Perfective is the marked member of the Perfective/ Imperfective opposition, but it cannot always be replaced by the Imperfective, i.e. the Perfective always has perfective meaning, whereas the Imperfective may or may not have imperfective meaning. We may

---

[1] This example is cited by Marchand (1955: 50), who provides a detailed comparison between Italian and Spanish, and English, in terms similar to those of this paragraph.

[2] Jakobson (1932: 74, 76) states explicitly that the marked member of a correlation must contain some feature that is absent in the unmarked member, though in later work on syntactic markedness the validity of this has been questioned, for instance by Růžička (1970). This line of analysis for Russian is developed more fully by Forsyth (1970).

illustrate this by examining one of the contexts where, in Russian, only the Perfective is possible, i.e. where it is not possible to use the Imperfective despite its unmarked character. In specifying how long it took for some event to come about, using the preposition *za* plus time expression 'in (so much time)', unless the reference is to a habitual event, only the Perfective is possible; an adverbial like *na ètot raz* 'on this occasion' excludes habituality. Thus to say 'on this occasion it took us five minutes to solve the problem', the Perfective is possible, the Imperfective excluded: *na ètot raz my rešili* (Pfv.)/*rešali* (Ipfv.) *zadaču za pjat' minut*. In general, however, even where, on other grounds, one might expect the Perfective to be used, it is possible in Russian to use the Imperfective, when there is no specific reference to the completeness of the event, in what has been called the constative general factual, or simple denotative meaning of the Imperfective.[1] Here the speaker is simply interested in expressing the bare fact that such and such an event did take place, without any further implications, and in particular without any implication of progressive or habitual meaning; sentence-stress falls on the verb. Thus, the question *vy čitali 'Vojnu i mir'?* 'have you read *War and Peace*?', and similarly the answer *čital* 'yes, I have', both with the Imperfective, simply enquire about and register the fact that the person in question has indeed read the book mentioned; whereas the Perfective *vy pročitali 'Vojnu i mir'?* is more specific, asking whether the addressee has finished *War and Peace*. An even clearer example would be the waiter's question *vy uže zakazyvali?* 'have you already ordered?', which is clearly neither progressive nor habitual in meaning, but where the Imperfective is still possible, in this general factual meaning. This is perhaps the strongest single piece of evidence in Russian (and similarly in the other Slavonic languages) for considering the Perfective to be the marked form. Incidentally, where the Imperfective and Perfective are explicitly contrasted, then the Imperfective may well take on the opposite semantic value of the Perfective, as in *on mnogo delal* (Ipfv.), *no malo sdelal* (Pfv.) 'he did (Ipfv., i.e. tried to do, undertook) a lot, but did (Pfv., i.e. accomplished) little';[2] but on its own, the Imperfective *delal* does not imply that the action was attempted but unsuccessful. The application of this particular criterion to many other aspectual oppositions such as Progressive/non-Progressive in English, or the Simple Past/

---

[1] Forsyth (1970: 82–102).
[2] Jakobson (1932: 74).

Imperfect in Spanish, or the Aorist/Imperfect distinction in Ancient Greek (and those Slavonic languages that retain these forms) is more problematic, since the usual pattern here is for the categories to be mutually exclusive, i.e. the replacement of an Aorist by an Imperfect or vice versa usually implies a different meaning altogether, not merely loss of some information by use of an unmarked category. It is generally, though not universally, assumed that in Romance and Slavonic languages, and in Georgian, it is the Aorist (Simple Past) that is the unmarked member of the Aorist/Imperfect opposition, but the possibility cannot be excluded that we are here dealing with two equally marked members of an equipollent opposition. Some of the other criteria mentioned below do, however, seem to point in the direction of the Aorist as the unmarked member of the opposition.[1]

6.2. Markedness and morphology

There are a number of morphological peculiarities that tend to correlate with the marked/unmarked distinction. For instance, unmarked categories tend to have less morphological material than marked categories. The Perfective/Imperfective opposition in Slavonic provides little evidence here, since it is possible both to form Perfectives from Imperfectives (primarily by prefixation), and also to form Imperfectives from Perfectives (by suffixation). On this criterion of extra morphological material, though, all of the following would be marked, which seems to correlate in general with the intuitive feeling about markedness: the English Progressive and Perfect; the Italian and Spanish Progressive; all of the suffixed aspect forms in Chinese, in contrast to the simple form of the verb; the Imperfective in Persian (with the prefix *mi-*; see section 6.5).

The second morphological criterion, the greater likelihood of morphological irregularity in unmarked forms, gives good results for the Aorist as an unmarked category in Indo-European languages (and

---

[1] For a treatment of the English Progressive as a marked category, see Hatcher (1951). The possibility of Spanish sentences like: *mientras duraron* (Simple Past) *en casa de Isidora las abundancias y el regalo, Mariano hizo la vida de señorito holgazán* (Pérez Galdós) 'while opulence and luxury continued at Isidora's, Mariano lived the life of an idle young gentleman', with the Simple Past in a time clause introduced by *mientras* 'while', rather than the expected Imperfect *duraban*, suggests that there may be grounds for considering the Simple Past as unmarked relative to the Imperfect.

equally for the Simple Past in the Romance languages).[1] Typically, Aorists are so irregular that they have to be learned as principal parts of verbs that do not follow the most regular patterns, whereas the Imperfect is usually predictable from the Present stem of the verb. In Slavonic, the Aorist can be characterised in the same way, while the Imperfect is usually regular in formation, and includes both a suffix and personal endings, while the Aorist often has only personal endings, which may be null.[2] Similarly, in Georgian the endings of the Imperfect are regular, and are attached to the stem after a suffix -*d*; while the Aorist forms are not always predictable from other forms, and may involve stem change rather than affixation.[3]

In the marked category, there is very often syncretism of forms that are kept apart in the unmarked category, or else certain forms are simply missing from the paradigm of the marked form. Thus in Russian, in the unmarked Imperfective there is a three-way tense distinction Present/Past/Future, while in the marked Perfective there is a two-way distinction Past/Future. In Italian, the marked Progressive form lacks a Future (**sarò scrivendo* 'I shall be writing'). In Arabic (table 3), the Imperfective has several homophonous forms, while the Perfective has none. These seem to be among the clearest examples of the application of this criterion to aspect, and elsewhere the results seem very marginal: thus in Spanish, for instance, the one form *hablaba* does duty for both first person singular and third person singular in the Imperfect, while in the Simple Past there are separate forms for all three persons and both numbers (in particular first singular *hablé* and third person singular *habló*), but the difference is slight, and is the kind of difference one could well imagine having arisen accidentally as a result of regular sound change.[4]

[1] All Romance Imperfects require a suffix (e.g. Spanish *ponía* 'I was putting', *hablaba* 'I was speaking'), while many Aorists do not, having instead a stem change (e.g. *puse* 'I put') or no change at all (e.g. *hablé* 'I spoke').

[2] E.g. Old Church Slavonic Imperfect *dělaaxъ* 'I was doing', *dělaaše* 'he was doing', Aorist *děla* 'he did'.

[3] E.g. Imperfect *çer-d-i* 'you were writing', *krep-d-i* 'you were picking', Aorist *çer-e* 'you wrote', *krip-e* 'you picked'.

[4] This is in fact the case, the Latin endings being -*am* and -*a* for first and third person respectively. In Italian, too, by regular sound change, one would expect a form *amava* for all three persons of the Imperfect of *amare* 'to love', but in fact in many dialects and the standard language the three forms are now distinguished as *amavo*, *amavi*, *amava*, where the first two persons have taken endings from other tenses/conjugations.

6.3. Neutralisation[1]

If we take a case where some verb or verbal form, because of its meaning or for other reasons, has morphologically only one aspectual form where other verbs or verbal forms have two or more, then one might expect the morphology of this verb to reflect that of the unmarked member of the opposition. Of course, there is another possibility, in the case of verbs which for semantic reasons have only one form, namely that the form that is appropriate semantically will be used. But we would not expect to find verbs with the morphology of the marked aspect being used irrespective of aspect, or only with the meaning of the unmarked aspect, at least not as a regular phenomenon. In Russian, there are several verbs that can be used without morphological change as both Perfective and Imperfective; among those listed by Forsyth[2] are the following: *velet'* 'command', *ženit'(sja)* 'marry', *kaznit'* 'execute', *ranit'* 'wound', *rodit'* 'give birth to', *rodit'sja* 'be born', *bežat'* 'flee', plus a large number of verbs of foreign origin in *-(iz)(ir)ovat'*, e.g. *atakovat'* 'attack', *telefonirovat'* 'telephone'. The only prefixed forms mentioned are *obeščat'* 'promise', which may well be felt to be a simple verb in the modern language (it has a colloquial Perfective *poobeščat'*), and has in any case the Church Slavonic imperfectivisation formation of replacing stem-final *-t* with *-šč* (for *-tj*), and *issledovat'* 'investigate', which has the imperfectivising suffix *-ovat'*. An interesting example of morphological neutralisation is provided by Georgian. Most Georgian verbs have distinct Aorist and Imperfect in the Past Tense, but some stative verbs lack this distinction, having only one form whose meaning (given the meaning of the verbs) is primarily like that of the Imperfective of other verbs. Yet morphologically, these forms are Aorists, e.g. *viqavi* 'I was', *vizine* 'I slept, was asleep', *viʒeki* 'I was sitting'.[3]

6.4. Markedness and frequency

One criterion that has not been mentioned so far in connection with markedness and aspect, although it seems an easy and objective criterion to apply, is frequency. The reason for this is that frequency is called into question as a valid criterion precisely by that language that otherwise provides one of the clearest examples of the marking con-

---

[1] In the Prague School treatment of markedness in phonology, neutralisation was the key criterion.
[2] 1970: 32–3.
[3] Vogt (1971: 182–3).

vention for aspect, namely Russian. In a detailed statistical analysis of both conversational and nonconversational material, Josselson[1] comes to the conclusion that in both kinds of style, the Perfective is in fact rather commoner overall than the Imperfective (in conversational style, 53.1:46.9; in nonconversational style, 57.5:42.5), and this is in spite of the fact that there is an Imperfective Present but no Perfective Present. Within the Past Tense, the Perfective is more frequent than the Imperfective by a factor of about three to one, while in the Future the predominance of the Perfective is even greater. Yet it is disturbing to have to dismiss frequency as a criterion in studying aspect, when elsewhere it seems to give such good results. In the remainder of this chapter we shall be referring to some features of markedness that may go some way towards explaining the apparent discrepancy that results from applying the frequency criterion in discussing aspect. In addition, it is possible that frequency may indeed be less valuable as a criterion in dealing with categories, like aspect, that are closely linked with meaning, in contrast to phonological segments, for instance, where there is no direct relation with anything semantic. Clearly the choice of aspect is very closely connected with what the speaker wants to say, in the sense that if, for instance, he wants to give a long piece of description of a scene, he will inevitably use far more Imperfectives in a language like Russian than if he were to give a piece of narrative with one event following another, and therefore a preponderance of Perfectives. In both cases, the ratio of the various segmental phonemes to one another would be little affected, especially over long stretches of text. Thus the preponderance of Perfective over Imperfective may well reflect the fact that speakers and writers are more likely to want to express those meanings that are associated with the Perfective Aspect. Even if, in analysing a language like Spanish, it is found that the Simple Past is more common than the Imperfect, this does not necessarily mean that the latter is marked, because on the basis of the Russian data we would expect a form with perfective meaning to be more frequent than one that is imperfective in meaning; though if the Simple Past is unmarked in Spanish, then one would expect a higher percentage of them in absolute terms than is found in Russian. And where a form occurs with clearly restricted frequency as against a form with similar meaning in other languages (such as the Italian and Spanish Progressives vis-à-vis the English Progressive), this seems to be good evidence for its being marked.

[1] 1953: 20–2.

6.5. Markedness and context

So far, it has been tacitly assumed that if an opposition is characterised by a markedness difference, then it will always be the case that the one member of the opposition will be unmarked. However, it is equally possible that in certain circumstances one member of an opposition will be unmarked, while in other circumstances the other member (or one of the other members) will be unmarked.[1]

The problem of morphological markedness in Russian, for instance, is rather more complex than suggested in the earlier discussion in this chapter, as may already be clear from the discussion of section 5.1.1 on the morphology of aspect in Russian. In certain cases, the Perfective has more morphological material than the Imperfective (if the Perfective is formed from an Imperfective by prefixation, with provisos concerning the exact semantic match between the members of such pairs, or if it is formed from the Imperfective by suffixation), while in others it is the Imperfective that has more morphological material (if the Imperfective is formed from a Perfective, typically a prefixed Perfective, by suffixation). In the modern language, the presence or absence of more morphological material does not affect the possibility of using the Imperfective as a general factual (cp. the pairs *čitat'*, Perfective *pročitat'*, 'read', and *zakazyvat'*, Perfective *zakazat'*, 'order', used as illustrations above), i.e. the Imperfective is in each case the unmarked form. However, there seem to be some facts that speak in favour of a differential treatment of markedness in the two cases. Thus it has been noted[2] that the use of the Imperfective as a general-factual is particularly common with nonprefixed verbs, and rather less common with Imperfective verbs that owe their imperfectivity to a suffix that derives them from a Perfective. Similarly in Bulgarian, the Imperfective Aorist is particularly common with simple Imperfective verbs, i.e. those that are not derived from Perfectives by suffixation.[3] It is conceivable that at some time in the history of the Russian language, markedness did correlate more closely with morphological markedness, i.e. that there were

---

[1] Compare the analysis in Sommerstein (1973: 96), modifying that of Chomsky and Halle (1968: 405–6), whereby in the phonological opposition voiced/voiceless, the voiceless member is unmarked in obstruents (stops and fricatives) and the voiced member is unmarked in sonorants (vowels, nasals, liquids).

[2] Rassudova (1968: 26–7).

[3] Further evidence of the relative rarity of suffixed Imperfectives in Russian, and even more so in Old Russian, is given by the statistics quoted in Forsyth (1972: 500).

unmarked verbal forms that were basically Imperfective if the verb had no prefix but Perfective if it had a prefix (i.e. a prefix that changed the meaning of the verb other than just aspectually), while all purely aspectual derived forms (both de-Imperfective Perfectives and de-Perfective Imperfectives) were marked, and that the present statistical imbalance between suffixed and nonsuffixed Imperfectives is a reflection of this earlier situation. A situation similar to the posited older Slavonic system may well still be in existence in Lithuanian: most simple (non-prefixed) verbs are Imperfective, and often have Perfective forms with prefixes (less commonly, suffixes); some prefixed verbs are Perfective, at least in certain tenses, and have marked Imperfective forms derived by suffixation where it is necessary to give overt expression of imperfective meaning. The important point to note is that markedness values can change diachronically, and that presumably there are intermediate stages where it is difficult or impossible to assign markedness, at least to the system as a whole.

Another place in Russian where present morphological complexity and low frequency seem to point to earlier markedness concerns the Imperfective Future, i.e. the periphrastic form with *budu* and the Infinitive. Even for verbs which have Perfectives formed by prefixation, the Imperfective Future contains more morphological material than the Perfective Future, and for verbs where the Imperfective is formed from the Perfective by suffixation the difference is even more apparent: compare *ja ub'ju* (Pfv.) and *ja budu ubivat'* (Ipfv.) 'I shall kill'. Yet by the replaceability criterion (the general factual meaning test), the Imperfective is still the unmarked member of the opposition. If, as is claimed here, markedness values can change diachronically, then it is not unnatural to assume that some of the usual concomitant features of markedness (such as more morphological material) may still reflect an earlier stage with different markedness values from those appertaining at a given moment.

We may now turn to the rather more complicated aspectual system of Bulgarian, where there are two formal oppositions: Perfective versus Imperfective and, in the Past Tense, Aorist versus Imperfect. We may ask which form is used, corresponding to the Russian general factual use of the Imperfective, when we are interested solely in establishing whether or not a given event took place. The answer is the Imperfective Aorist, e.g. *kupuvax si učebnik* 'I have bought/did buy a textbook'. This suggests that the unmarked member of the Perfective/Imperfective opposition is the Imperfective (as in Russian), and the unmarked member of the Aorist/Imperfect opposition the Aorist (as it probably is generally in the Indo-European languages). The same assignment of markedness has been suggested for Georgian,[1] with the Imperfective Aorist doubly unmarked and the Perfective Imperfect doubly marked. So far, however, we have been considering the two relevant oppositions separately, and when we come to combining them it is not clear that one is justified in following Vogt in making the Imperfective Aorist the least marked, the Perfective Imperfect the most marked, with the Perfective Aorist and the Imperfective Imperfect as intermediate categories. For when we look at combinations of aspects in Bulgarian and Georgian, we find that the most usual forms are precisely the Perfective Aorist and the Imperfective Imperfect, while the other possibilities always carry some special or other meaning: the Perfective Imperfect typically carries habitual meaning, while the Imperfective Aorist in Bulgarian often has general factual meaning. The assignment of markedness in languages like Bulgarian and Georgian is therefore much more complicated than in, say, Russian: on the one hand, Imperfective is overall less marked than Perfective, and Aorist is overall less marked than Imperfect; but in combination with the Imperfect, Imperfective is less marked than Perfective, while in combination with the Aorist, Perfective is less marked than Imperfective; similarly, in combination with the Imperfective, Imperfect is less marked than Aorist, while in combination with the Perfective, Aorist is less marked than Imperfect. Here, then, markedness values are also affected by the value of other aspectual parameters in context, in addition to being established in absolute terms for the system as a whole.

Another case where assignment of markedness can be affected by the rest of the context, in a number of languages, concerns the interaction of aspect and tense (or time reference, where tense is not present as an overt category). In the course of this book we have noted a number of correlations between past tense (or time reference) and perfective aspect on the one hand and present tense (or time reference) and imperfective aspect on the other (see especially section 4.5), for instance in those African languages where the Perfective forms of verbs are interpreted, in the absence of indication to the contrary, as past, while Imperfective forms are taken to be present; and in Indo-European, where we have evidence of an earlier stage with an aspectual opposition

[1] Vogt (1971: 186–7).

between Perfective (Aorist) and Imperfective (Present) stems, with the Perfective normally having past time reference, and the Imperfective having present time reference. In section 6.4 we noted that in the Past Tense in Russian, the Perfective is far more frequent than the Imperfective, even though in the system overall it is the Imperfective that is unmarked; the Present Tense can only be Imperfective. Thus in combination with past tense there is generally in languages a tendency for the perfective aspect to be unmarked, while with present tense the tendency is for imperfective aspect to be unmarked. The aspectual system of Persian is interesting in this light.[1] The overt aspectual difference is between a Perfective with no marker and an Imperfective with the prefix *mi-*. Morphologically, then, the *mi-*less form would appear to be unmarked, and in the Past Tense this seems in fact to be the case, corresponding to the general tendency for past to be perfective. Moreover, a small number of verbs which by their meaning would appear to favour Imperfective rather than Perfective Aspect in fact have *mi-*less forms only, even when they are clearly Imperfective, e.g. *dāštan* 'to have', and some forms of *budan* 'to be'. In the Present Tense, apart from these few verbs, all Persian verbs occur only with the prefix *mi-*.[2] In the Present Tense it would be strange to speak of the Imperfective forms in *mi-* as being marked, since they do not in fact contrast with any other aspectual value, let alone being marked relative to one. With the prefix *mi-* having become in the modern language a general marker of Imperfective Aspect, there is no longer any absolute correlation between morphological markedness (presence of *mi-*) and markedness within the aspectual system, where the Imperfective is unmarked within the Present Tense. Thus, as to some extent with suffixed Imperfectives in Slavonic languages, the morphological form bears witness to an earlier stage of the language, when the *mi-* prefix was coming into general use and was a marked form. If we accept that in languages like the Romance languages and Ancient Greek the Aorist is unmarked vis-à-vis the Imperfect, then we are by no means committed to generalising this markedness assignment to other tenses, indeed the absence of separate forms with perfective meaning in the Present prevents us from doing so. In Ancient Greek, furthermore, it

---

[1] For the data, cp. Lambton (1957: 16–17, 25–6, 143–51).
[2] The equivalent forms without *mi-* can occur, but they either have habitual meaning, especially in slightly older Persian, or have become confused with the Subjunctive, i.e. have modal rather than aspectual value.

would not be necessary for the Aorist (perfective meaning) nonfinite forms to be unmarked relative to their Present (imperfective meaning) counterparts.

Those African languages (see section 4.5) where the morphologically unmarked form of a stative verb is taken to be imperfective, but of a nonstative verb to be perfective, suggest a similar correlation between imperfective and stative, and between perfective and nonstative.

Another application of markedness relative to context would be to consider whether, for the expression of a given meaning, one or other aspect is the more usual. In Russian, for instance, although one can say either *ja zakazyval* (Ipfv.) *boršč* or *ja zakazal* (Pfv.) *boršč* for 'I ordered borshch', i.e. without any implication of imperfectivity, it could be argued that in order to express this situation the Perfective is the unmarked form, while the Imperfective will always add some special nuance, for instance general factual meaning.

6.6. Degrees of markedness

In this section we have considered the marked/unmarked distinction firstly as it characterises aspectual oppositions within the aspectual system as a whole; then as it may function relativised to certain contexts (such as other aspectual values, tense, stativity, sense to be conveyed). Finally, it may be noted that the degree of markedness of a marked form need not always be the same. In Spanish, for instance, both the Imperfect and the Past Progressive are marked forms relative to the Simple Past, but the Past Progressive is even more marked than the Imperfect (it can be replaced by the latter); similarly, the Spanish Progressive is more marked relative to the non-Progressive than is the English Progressive, while the French progressive paraphrase (*être en train de* . . .) is more marked than either of these.

APPENDIX A

Language guide

A.1. **Genetic classification of languages cited**

Table 6 gives a genetic classification of all the languages cited in the present book, including those only mentioned in passing. Some less well established genetic groupings (e.g. between Uralic and Turkic) have not been taken into account.

Table 6. *Genetic classification of languages cited*

Indo-European
  Hittite
  Indo-Iranian
    Indic: Sanskrit, Hindi, Urdu, Punjabi
    Iranian: Persian
  Balto-Slavonic
    Baltic: Lithuanian, Latvian (Lettish)
    Slavonic (Slavic)
      South Slavonic: Old Church Slavonic (Old Bulgarian), Bulgarian, Macedonian, Serbo-Croatian
      East Slavonic: Russian
      West Slavonic: Czech, Polish, Upper Sorbian (Upper Lusatian, Upper Wendish)
  Albanian
  Hellenic: Ancient Greek, Modern Greek
  Italic
    Latin
    Romance: Italian, French, Spanish, Portuguese, Romanian
  Celtic: Irish, Scots Gaelic, Welsh
  Germanic: Gothic, German, Dutch, English, Icelandic
Uralic
  Finno-Ugric
    Ugric: Hungarian, Vogul (Mańśi)
    Finno-Permic: Finnish, Estonian, Cheremis (Mari), Zyryan (Komi), Votyak (Udmurt)
  Samoyedic: Nenets (Yurak Samoyed)

Table 6. *Genetic classification of languages cited* (*cont.*)
Turkic: Turkish
South Caucasian (Kartvelian): Georgian
Semitic: Akkadian, Arabic
Sino-Tibetan: (Mandarin) Chinese
Niger–Congo
    Mande: Kpelle
    Kwa: Fante (Akan), Yoruba, Igbo
    Bantu: Swahili, Shona, ChiBemba

A.2. **Aspectual systems of individual languages**

The purpose of this section is to bring together, in summary form with bibliographical references, a description of the various aspects that have been discussed in different parts of this book, in those languages which have formed the backbone of the material used in this book. The sections on English and the Slavonic languages Russian and Bulgarian are rather more detailed than the others, since English is the language familiar to all readers of this book, while the Slavonic languages have played an important role in the development of the study of aspect. For fuller details, reference should be made to the appropriate sections of this book, and to the works listed below.

A.2.1. *English*

English has two aspectual oppositions that pervade the whole of the verbal system, that between Progressive (verb *to be* and verbal form in *-ing*) and non-Progressive, and that between Perfect (verb *to have* and Past Participle) and non-Perfect. With nonstative verbs the difference between Progressive and non-Progressive is in general that between progressive and nonprogressive meaning. However, this formal opposition is also found with stative verbs, in English, as opposed to many other languages with a similar opposition, and here the meaning distinction is usually that between a temporally restricted state (Progressive) and a temporally unrestricted state (non-Progressive). The difference between Perfect and non-Perfect is that between perfect meaning and nonperfect meaning, although the Pluperfect and Future Perfect can also indicate relative time reference. In addition, in the Past Tense only, English has a separate Habitual, using the auxiliary *used to*; this form is replaceable by the non-Habitual equivalent, i.e. the non-Habitual does not exclude habitual meaning.

A recent handbook dealing with English aspect (and other verbal categories) from a practical rather than a theoretical viewpoint is Leech (1971), which contains a bibliography. Recent key works in the development of the study of aspect in English include Ota (1963), Joos (1964), Palmer (1965), and Allen (1966). Particular attention has been attracted to the Progressive, which is lacking in many of the other major European languages. Schopf (1974a) reprints a number of articles on the Progressive in English, viewed both synchronically and diachronically, as well as an original essay by the editor (Schopf 1974b) on recent approaches to the analysis of the Progressive in English; this reader also contains a number of more general articles on aspect, and articles originally written in English are reprinted without being translated into German. Other key works dealing exclusively or primarily with the Progressive are Hatcher (1951), Nehls (1974), and Scheffer (1975).

A.2.2.   *Slavonic*

A.2.2.1.   Russian
          There is an aspectual opposition between Perfective and Imperfective. In general, simple verbs are Imperfective (e.g. *pisat'* 'write'); prefixed derivatives of simple verbs are Perfective (e.g. *napisat'* 'write', *vypisat'* 'copy out'); and suffixed derivatives of Perfective verbs are again Imperfective (e.g. *vypisyvat'* 'copy out').

The aspectual opposition exists in the Past Tense. In the non-Past, there is a distinction in the Imperfective between Present and Future, the latter a periphrastic formation using *budu* with the Infinitive. There is only one non-Past Perfective form, which usually has future time reference, and is traditionally called the Perfective Future.

The fullest account of Russian aspect available in English is Forsyth (1970), with bibliography. Those who read German should also consult Isačenko (1962: 347–418). A recent work in the native Russian tradition is Bondarko (1971). Key contributions to the development of the analysis of Russian aspect include Mazon (1914) and Jakobson (1932). Bartschat (1974) is a discussion of some recent approaches to aspect in Russian and the other Slavonic languages.

A.2.2.2.   Bulgarian
          The aspectual system of Bulgarian is considerably more complex than that of Russian. In addition to the opposition between

Perfective (with perfective meaning) and Imperfective (with imperfective meaning or neutral between perfective and imperfective meaning), there is an opposition in the Past Tense only between Imperfect and Aorist. The Imperfect has imperfective meaning and the Aorist has perfective meaning; such combinations as Perfective Imperfect and Imperfective Aorist are possible, and either represent combinations of different submeanings of perfective and imperfective meaning, or, in the case of the Imperfective Aorist, can also represent the combination of perfective meaning (whence Aorist) with aspectually unspecified meaning (whence Imperfective). In addition, there is an opposition between Perfect and non-Perfect, in all tenses and in both Perfective and Imperfective Aspect. There is a three-way tense distinction: Present/Past/Future, and each tense has both Perfective and Imperfective, both Perfect and non-Perfect forms.

The standard descriptive work is Maslov (1959). A bibliography of the major works is given by Walter (1973:198); to this list one might add Andrejczin (1938), and Ivanova (1974).

A.2.2.3.   Old Church Slavonic

For Old Church Slavonic, with an aspectual system similar to that of Bulgarian except for a less well developed Perfective/Imperfective opposition, the classical treatment is Dostál (1954); for a more recent discussion, see Amse-de Jong (1974).

A.2.3.   *Romance*

A useful introduction to aspect in the Romance languages is Klein (1974: chapters 4, 5), with bibliography.

A.2.3.1.   French

In written French, there is a three-way formal distinction among the past tenses: Past Definite (with perfective meaning, e.g. *j'écrivis* 'I wrote'), Imperfect (with imperfective meaning, e.g. *j'écrivais* 'I was writing, I used to write'), and Perfect (with perfect meaning, e.g. *j'ai écrit* 'I have written'). The opposition between Past Definite and Imperfect is restricted to the Past Tense, while there are Perfect forms for all tenses. Semantically this is not a three-way opposition, but rather two binary oppositions: perfective/nonperfective and perfect/nonperfect, although within the Perfect there is no overt expression of the perfective/imperfective semantic distinction. In spoken French, the Past Definite is not used, and the Perfect (also called Compound Past) is used in both senses.

The standard treatment of the French verbal forms is Imbs (1960). A recent theoretical treatment is Pollak (1960), which also contains a review of earlier work on aspect in French and in Latin (chapter 11); see also Garey (1957), Harris (1971).

A.2.3.2. Spanish

Spanish has the same formal distinctions as written French, although the semantic distinction between Simple Past (corresponding to the French Past Definite, e.g. *escribí* 'I wrote') and Perfect (e.g. *he escrito* 'I have written'), in particular, is somewhat different; see Bull (1963), Barrera-Vidal (1972). In addition, Spanish has separate Progressive forms (e.g. *estoy escribiendo* 'I am writing') with progressive meaning, while the equivalent non-Progressive forms (e.g. *escribo* 'I write') do not exclude progressive meaning.

A.2.4. *Greek*

A.2.4.1. Ancient Greek

In addition to the opposition between Perfect (e.g. *léluka* 'I have loosed') and non-Perfect, Ancient Greek has, within the non-Perfect forms, an opposition between Aorist (e.g. *élūsa* 'I loosed') and non-Aorist (e.g. Imperfect *élūon* 'I was loosing, I used to loose'). In the Indicative Mood, the Aorist is essentially a Past Tense, and this particular aspectual distinction does not exist in the other tenses; in the other moods and in nonfinite forms, the distinction between Aorist and non-Aorist is purely aspectual (perfective versus imperfective meaning).

A traditional description of the Ancient Greek verbal forms is Goodwin (1889). For more recent discussions, see Holt (1943), Lyons (1963: 111–19), and Friedrich (1974).

A.2.4.2. Modern Greek

Modern Greek has a Perfective/Imperfective opposition running through all tenses, moods, and nonfinite forms. In addition, within the Perfective, there are distinct Perfect forms. For the forms and their meanings, see Seiler (1952).

A.2.5. *Chinese (Mandarin)*

Chinese has a number of verbal suffixes with aspectual, or combined aspectual and temporal, value, for instance Progressive *-zhe*, Perfective *-le* (the latter combining perfective meaning and relative past time reference). For the use of these particles, see Jaxontov (1957). For those who do not read Russian, Chao (1968), though oriented towards the formal distinctions rather than their meanings, also gives useful indications of the meanings of the various suffixes.

A.2.6. *Other languages*

The following should also be of interest, even to readers not familiar with the languages described, from the viewpoint of the general theory of aspect.

Although Turkish has not been discussed in detail in this book, there is a rather rich literature on aspect in Turkish, a recent work being Johanson (1971), with bibliography. For a comparison of aspect in Slavonic languages and in Turkish, see Koschmieder (1953).

The Bantu language with the richest set of tense and aspect oppositions seems to be ChiBemba, described in Givón (1972: chapter 4, especially pp. 174–9 and 206–13).

APPENDIX B

Recent approaches to aspect

The basic aim of this book has been to introduce the reader to the concept of aspect, illustrating this with examples from languages likely to be familiar and some which are probably unfamiliar. As such, there has been no systematic attempt to describe or evaluate recent, less well established approaches to the problem of aspect. In this appendix, three such recent approaches are referred to and characterised in general terms; the characterisations are not detailed, and readers interested in these approaches will naturally want to refer to the cited references for themselves. Of the three approaches, model-theoretic semantics presupposes some knowledge of formal logic, although of the two references cited below, Dowty (1972) contains much that is of general interest even to those not interested primarily in model-theoretic semantics. The references cited on feature analysis are fairly technical, but not unduly so. The works on the localist theory of aspect should be understandable with a general background in linguistics and the knowledge of aspect gained from the present book. The three approaches presented are very different from one another,[1] and will give some idea of the range of theoretical approaches to aspect, in addition to those of traditional grammar, that are to be found in current work.

B.1. Localist theory of aspect

In section 5.2.1, we noted similarities in a wide range of languages between the formal structures used to express locative meaning and those used to express progressive meaning, or more generally imperfective meaning. On the basis of these and similar observations,

---

[1] For instance, both Anderson (1973) and Haltof (1968) are conceived within the overall framework of generative grammar, but are otherwise radically different; moreover, neither localist theory nor feature analysis presupposes a generative framework.

Anderson (1973) proposes a localist theory of aspect, whereby progressive meaning is represented semantically in the same terms as a
locative construction, e.g. *the man is falling* as *the man is in the process
of the man falling* (p. 72). This is part of a more general localist approach
to language, whereby various apparently nonlocative constructions are
represented in localist terms. Anderson illustrates the formal parallels
between locative and aspectual constructions in a wide range of languages
(though he does not discuss the discrepancies that are found in many of
these languages, as noted in section 5.2.1 above), but does not give a
detailed analysis of any one language in these terms. Such an analysis of
Russian is provided by Miller (1972), who represents Imperfective
Aspect as *being in a situation*, while the Perfective Aspect also obtains
a localist representation, which combines entry into a situation, being in
the situation, and exit from the situation. This corresponds closely to
our discussion in section 0.1 and passim, where the imperfective is
described as viewing a situation from inside, whereas the perfective
views it from outside, without discriminating beginning, middle, and
end. There is one discrepancy between Anderson's and Miller's use of
locative representations: Anderson claims that being in a situation
characterises essentially progressive meaning, with extension beyond
this, e.g. to imperfective meaning in general, being secondary; whereas
for Miller, being in a situation characterises imperfective meaning as a
whole. Semantically, it would seem that Miller's approach is more
adequate, although the formal parallelism between progressive and
locative seems to be much commoner that that between imperfective
and locative across the languages of the world, a point in favour of
Anderson. For further discussion, see Comrie (1975a).

B.2. **Feature analysis**

  The use of terms like perfective, imperfective, in isolation
tends to disguise the fact that the aspectual system of a language is not
just a set of discrete entities, each equally distinct from each other one,
but rather a set of oppositions, so that strictly we have an opposition
between Perfective and Imperfective in Russian, for instance, there
being no third term in Russian. Such a binary opposition can be represented in terms of a binary feature, [$\pm$ PERFECTIVE], i.e. Perfective forms
are characterised by the feature value [+PERFECTIVE], Imperfective
forms by the feature value [$-$PERFECTIVE]. Since in this case the Imperfective is the unmarked member of the opposition, we can characterise

the Imperfective as [u PERFECTIVE], the Perfective as [m PERFECTIVE], where *u* means unmarked and *m* means marked, and have a rule to tell us that [u PERFECTIVE] is [− PERFECTIVE] (whence the opposite markedness value, [m PERFECTIVE], is [+ PERFECTIVE]), in this case.

So far, the use of features in this section has been little more than a recapitulation of the formal opposition. Where, however, the relations between the formal oppositions is more complex than with the Perfective/Imperfective opposition in Russian, the use of features can help to show the relations among the various forms. In Ancient Greek, for instance, the non-Perfect forms of the Indicative Mood are the Aorist, Imperfect, Present, and Future. The relations among the forms are that the Aorist and Imperfect are both past tenses, while the Present and Future are not; among the nonpast tenses, the Future is a future tense, while the Present is not. The aspectual distinction perfective/imperfective also exists, the Aorist being perfective, the Imperfect and Present being imperfective, while the Future is aspectually neutral. With the aid of three binary features, [± PAST], [± FUTURE],[1] and [± PERFECTIVE] the four forms can be characterised as follows, thus bringing out the relations that hold among the forms but are not necessarily given overt expression in their morphology:

Aorist	[+PERFECTIVE, + PAST, − FUTURE]
Imperfect	[−PERFECTIVE, + PAST, − FUTURE]
Present	[−PERFECTIVE, − PAST, − FUTURE]
Future	[− PAST, + FUTURE]

Here, the use of features does not simply recapitulate the formal oppositions, but serves to show the nonformal relations that hold among the various forms.

A further degree of abstraction is introduced if the features are explicitly semantic, particularly within a framework which does not accept that the relation between formal and semantic categories is necessarily one-one or almost one-one. An instructive example of this approach is given in Haltof (1968),[2] which examines the relations between various semantic features and the Perfective/Imperfective opposition in Russian. The formal opposition is between the two categories Perfective and Imperfective, but in the semantic characterisa-

---

[1] It is not relevant to the present argument whether tense is treated as two binary oppositions, or as a single ternary opposition Present/Past/Future.
[2] See also Haltof (1967), Haltof and Steube (1970), and Walter (1973) for other applications of this approach.

tion of this opposition Haltof uses eight binary features, including, for instance, [ITERATIVE], [STATIVE]. Different combinations of these features lead to different choices between semantic and formal categories, so that there is no simple correlation between semantic and formal categories, rather the two are mediated by a more complex set of rules. The semantic features are typically arranged hierarchically, so that in the presence of both a dominating and a dominated feature it is the dominating feature that is decisive.[1]

B.3. **Model-theoretic semantics**

The model-theoretic approach to semantics attempts to go beyond the analysis of meaning in terms of semantic representations, since semantic representations are themselves formal objects that, strictly speaking, are still in need of interpretation.[2] Model-theoretic semantics looks at truth-functional relations between semantic representations of sentences: for instance, do two sentences necessarily have the same truth-value (i.e. is the one true whenever the other is true and false whenever the other is false), does one sentence necessarily imply another (thus if p implies q, then whenever p is true q must be true, but if p is false then q may be either true or false), etc.[3]

Dowty (1972) applies model-theoretic semantics to an analysis of aspect in English, though it should be noted that he does not apply the term 'aspect' directly to any particular formal oppositions of English, but rather to 'such distinctions as the beginning versus the duration of a state and the completion versus the imperfective duration of an act'

---

[1] Another model of aspect selection in terms of semantic features is presented by Pettersson (1972), again for Russian. This uses far fewer features: aspect selection is determined entirely by the features [±ACTIVITY] and [±TIME] (the latter being relevant only with [+ACTIVITY]), so that little advantage is gained from having distinct semantic and formal categories. Moreover, the model is difficult to evaluate since the author gives no adequate criteria for the assignment of feature values. See further Haltof (1974), Comrie (1975b).

[2] For the model-theoretic approach to linguistic semantics, see, for instance, Keenan (1972).

[3] 'Necessarily' is essential since the relevant notion is 'truth in any possible world', rather than just 'truth'. In our world it happens to be the ¦case that *John is in Paris* and *John is in the capital of France* have the same truth-value (either both are true, or both are false), but this is only because Paris happens to be the capital of France; if the capital of France were to be moved to some other city, then the two sentences would have different truth-values.

(p. 12). A model-theoretic analysis of the Russian Perfective/Imperfective opposition is given by Hoepelman (1974). One problem with the application of this kind of analysis to aspect in the sense in which it is understood in this textbook is that aspectual oppositions are often subjective rather than objective, i.e. do not necessarily lead to differences in truth-value, unless the speaker's view of the situation described is also included in the semantic representation.

REFERENCES

Agrell, S. (1908). 'Aspektänderung und Aktionsartbildung beim polnischen Zeitworte: ein Beitrag zum Studium der indogermanischen Präverbia und ihrer Bedeutungsfunktionen', *Lunds Universitets Årsskrift*, new series, **1**, IV. 2.

Allen, R. L. (1966). *The verb system of present-day American English*. The Hague: Mouton.

Amse-de Jong, T. H. (1974) *The meaning of the finite verb forms in the Old Church Slavonic Codex Suprasliensis: a synchronic study*. The Hague: Mouton.

Anderson, J. (1973). *An essay concerning aspect*. The Hague: Mouton.

Andrejczin, L. [= Andrejčin, L.] (1938). *Kategorie znaczeniowe koniugacji bułgarskiej*. Kraków: Polska Akademia Umiejętności.

Ashton, E. O. (1947). *Swahili grammar*. Second ed. London: Longman.

Barrera-Vidal, A. (1972). *Parfait simple et parfait composé en castillan moderne*. Munich: Hueber.

Bartschat, B. (formerly Haltof, B.) (1974). 'Die Behandlung des Verbalaspekts auf dem VII. Internationalen Slawistenkongress in Warschau', *Zeitschrift für Slawistik* **19**, 475–88.

Beaulieux, L. and Mladenov, S. (1950). *Grammaire de la langue bulgare*. Second ed. Paris: Institut d'Études slaves.

Bondarko, A. V. (1971). *Vid i vremja russkogo glagola (značenie i upotreblenie)*. Moscow: Prosveščenie.

Borras, F. M. and Christian, R. F. (1971). *Russian syntax: aspects of modern Russian syntax and vocabulary*. Second ed. Oxford: Clarendon Press.

Bull, W. E. (1963). *Time, tense, and the verb: a study in theoretical and applied linguistics, with particular attention to Spanish*. University of California Publications in Linguistics **19**.

Chao, Y. R. (1968). *A grammar of spoken Chinese*. Berkeley and Los Angeles: University of California Press.

Chomsky, N. (1971). 'Deep structure, surface structure, and semantic interpretation'. In D. D. Steinberg and L. A. Jakobovits, eds., *Semantics*. Cambridge: Cambridge University Press. Pp. 183–216.

Chomsky, N. and Halle, M. (1968). *The sound pattern of English*. New York: Harper and Row.

Comrie, B. (1975a). Review of Anderson (1973), *Lingua* **37**, 89–92.

Comrie, B. (1975b). Review of Pettersson (1973), *Modern Language Review*, **70**, 470–1.

Dambriūnas, L. (1959). 'Verbal aspects in Lithuanian', *Lingua Posnaniensis* **7**, 253–62. List of corrections in *Lingua Posnaniensis* **8** (1960), 361.

Denison, N. (1957). *The partitive in Finnish*. Annales Academiae Scientiarum Fennicae, Series B, **108**.

Dostál, A. (1954). *Studie o vidovém systému v staroslověnštině.* Prague: SNP.

Dowty, D. R. (1972). *Studies in the logic of verb aspect and time reference in English.* Studies in Linguistics **1**, Department of Linguistics, University of Texas at Austin.

Einarsson, S. (1949). *Icelandic: grammar, texts, glossary.* Baltimore: Johns Hopkins Press.

Ferrell, J. (1953). 'On the aspects of *byt′* and on the position of the periphrastic imperfective future in contemporary literary Russian', *Word* **9**, 362–76.

Forsyth, J. (1970). *A grammar of aspect: usage and meaning in the Russian verb.* Cambridge: Cambridge University Press.

Forsyth, J. (1972). 'The nature and development of the aspectual opposition in the Russian verb', *Slavonic and East European Review* **50** (121), 493–506.

Friedrich, P. (1974). 'On aspect theory and Homeric aspect', *International Journal of American Linguistics* **40**, 4, part 2.

Garey, H. B. (1957). 'Verbal aspect in French', *Language* **33**, 91–110.

Gildersleeve, B. L. and Lodge, G. (1895). *Latin grammar.* Third ed. London: Macmillan.

Givón, T. (1972) *Studies in ChiBemba and Bantu grammar.* Studies in African Linguistics, supplement 3.

Goodwin, W. W. (1889). *Syntax of the moods and tenses of the Greek verb.* Revised ed. London: Macmillan.

Goodwin, W. W. (1894). *A Greek grammar.* New ed. London: Macmillan.

Greenberg, J. H. (1966). *Language universals, with special reference to feature hierarchies.* The Hague: Mouton.

Grice, H. P. (1975). 'Logic and conversation'. In P. Cole and J. L. Morgan, eds. *Speech acts.* Syntax and Semantics **3**. New York: Academic Press. Pp. 41–58.

Haltof, B. (see also Bartschat, B.) (1967). 'Die Aspekte des modernen Russischen: Versuch einer semantischen und distributiven Modellierung', *Zeitschrift für Slawistik* **12**, 735–43.

Haltof, B. (1968). 'Ein semantisches Modell zur Aspektdeterminierung im modernen Russischen'. In *Probleme der strukturellen Grammatik und Semantik.* Leipzig: Karl Marx Universität. Pp. 133–50.

Haltof, B. (1974). Review of Pettersson (1973), *Zeitschrift für Slawistik* **18**, 104–16.

Haltof, B. and Steube, A. (1970). 'Zur semantischen Charakterisierung der Tempora im Russischen und Deutschen', *Linguistische Arbeitsberichte* **1**, 37–52.

Harris, M. B. (1971). 'The verbal systems of Latin and French' *Transactions of the Philological Society 1970*, Pp. 62–90.

Harrison, W. (1967). *The expression of the passive voice.* Studies in the modern Russian language **4**. Cambridge: Cambridge University Press.

Hatcher, A. G. (1951). 'The use of the progressive form in English: a new approach', *Language* **27**, 254–80.

Havránek, B. (1939). 'Aspects et temps du verbe en vieux slave'. In *Mélanges de linguistique offerts à Charles Bally.* Geneva: Georg. Pp. 223–30.

Hoepelman, J. Ph. (1974). 'Tense-logic and the semantics of the Russian aspects', *Theoretical Linguistics* **1**, 158–80.

Holt, J. (1943). *Études d'aspect.* Acta Jutlandica 15.2.

Imbs, P. (1960). *L'emploi des temps verbaux en français moderne: essai de grammaire descriptive.* Paris: Klincksieck.

Isačenko, A. V. (1962). *Die russische Sprache der Gegenwart*, part 1, *Formenlehre.* Halle (Saale): Niemeyer.

Ivanova, K. (1974). *Načini na glagolnoto dejstvie v səvremennija bəlgarski ezik.* Sofia: BAN.

References

Jakobson, R. (1932). 'Zur Struktur des russichen Verbums'. In *Charisteria G. Mathesio*. Prague: Cercle Linguistique de Prague. Pp. 74–84.

Jaxontov, S. E. (1957). *Kategorija glagola v kitajskom jazyke*. Leningrad: Izd-vo Leningradskogo universiteta.

Jespersen, O. (1924). *The philosophy of grammar*. London: George Allen and Unwin.

Johanson, L. (1971). *Aspekt im Türkischen*. Studia Turcica Upsaliensia **1**.

Joos, M. (1964). *The English verb: form and meanings*. Madison and Milwaukee: University of Wisconsin Press.

Josselson, H. H. (1953). *The Russian word count and frequency analysis of grammatical categories of Standard Literary Russian*. Detroit: Wayne University Press.

Keenan, E. L. (1972). 'On semantically based grammar', *Linguistic Inquiry* **3**, 413–61.

Klein, H. G. (1974). *Tempus, Aspekt, Aktionsart*. Tübingen: Niemeyer.

Koschmieder, E. (1953). 'Das türkische Verbum und der slavische Verbalaspekt'. In *Münchener Beiträge zur Slavenkunde, Festgabe für Paul Diels*. Munich: Isar-Verlag. Pp. 137–49.

Kuryłowicz, J. (1964). *The inflectional categories of Indo-European*. Heidelberg: Carl Winter.

Kuryłowicz, J. (1973). 'Verbal aspect in Semitic'. In *Gelb volume: Approaches to the study of the Ancient Near East*. Orientalia **42**, fascicules 1–2. Pp. 114–20.

Lakoff, G. (1966). 'Stative adjectives and verbs in English'. In *NSF-Report* **17**, Computational Laboratory, Harvard University.

Lambton, A. K. S. (1957). *Persian Grammar*. Corrected ed. Cambridge: Cambridge University Press.

Lancelot, C. and Arnauld, A. (1660). *Grammaire générale et raisonée*. Paris: Pierre le Petit.

Leech, G. N. (1971). *Meaning and the English verb*. London: Longman.

Lönngren, L. (1973). 'O protivopostavlenii aorističeskogo i perfektnogo značenij u russkogo glagola', *Scandoslavica* **19**, 103–10.

Lewis, G. L. (1967). *Turkish grammar*. Oxford: Clarendon Press.

Lyons, J. (1963). *Structural semantics*. Oxford: Basil Blackwell, for the Philological Society.

Lyons, J. (1968). *Introduction to theoretical linguistics*. Cambridge: Cambridge University Press.

Lytkin, V. I. and Timušev, D. A. (1961). 'Kratkij očerk grammatiki komi jazyka'. In *Komi-russkij slovar'*. Moscow: GIINS. Pp. 837–923.

McCawley, J. D. (1971). 'Tense and time reference in English'. In C. J. Fillmore and D. T. Langendoen, eds., *Studies in linguistic semantics*. New York: Holt, Rinehart and Winston. Pp. 96–113.

Majtinskaja, K. E. (1959). *Vengerskij jazyk*. II, *Grammatičeskoe slovoobrazovanie*. Moscow: Izd-vo AN SSSR.

Marchand, H. (1955). 'On a question of aspect: a comparison between the progressive form in English and that of Italian and Spanish', *Studia Linguistica* **9**, 45–52.

Maslov, Ju. S. (1959) 'Glagol'nyj vid v sovremennom bolgarskom literaturnom jazyke (značenie i upotreblenie)'. In S. B. Bernštejn, ed., *Voprosy grammatiki bolgarskogo literaturnogo jazyka*. Moscow: Izd-vo AN SSSR. Pp. 157–312.

Maslov, Ju. S. (1962a). Ed. *Voprosy glagol'nogo vida: sbornik*. Moscow: Izd-vo inostrannoj literatury.

Maslov, Ju. S. (1962b). 'Voprosy glagol'nogo vida v sovremennom zarubežnom jazykoznanii'. In Maslov (1962a), pp. 7–32.

Matthews, P. H. (1974). *Morphology: an introduction to the theory of word-structure*. Cambridge: Cambridge University Press.

Mazon, A. (1914). *Emplois des aspects du verbe russe.* Paris: Champion.

Miller, J. (1972). 'Towards a generative semantic account of aspect in Russian', *Journal of Linguistics* **8**, 217–36.

Nehls, D. (1974). *Synchron-diachrone Untersuchungen zur Expanded form im Englischen.* Munich: Hueber.

Ota, A. (1963). *Tense and aspect of present-day American English.* Tokyo: Kenkyusha.

Palmer, F. R. (1965). *A linguistic study of the English verb.* London: Longman.

Pettersson, T. (1972). *On Russian predicates: a theory of case and aspect.* Stockholm: Almqvist and Wiksell.

Pollak, W. (1960). *Studien zum 'Verbalaspekt' im Französischen.* Österreichische Akademie der Wissenschaften, **233**, treatise 5.

Quirk, R., Greenbaum, S., Leech, G., and Svartvik, J. (1972). *A grammar of contemporary English.* London: Longman.

Rassudova, O. P. (1968). *Upotreblenie vidov glagola v russkom jazyke.* Moscow: Izd-vo Moskovskogo universiteta.

Rowlands, E. C. (1969). *Teach yourself Yoruba.* London: English Universities Press

Růžička, R. (1970). 'Die Begriffe "merkmalhaltig" und "merkmallos" und ihre Verwendung in der generativen Transformationsgrammatik'. In K. H. Heidolph, M. Bierwisch, eds., *Progress in linguistics.* The Hague: Mouton. Pp. 260–85.

Scheffer, J. (1975). *The progressive in English.* Amsterdam: North Holland.

Schopf, A. (1974a). Ed. *Der englische Aspekt.* Darmstadt: Wissenschaftliche Buchgesellschaft.

Schopf, A. (1974b). 'Neuere Arbeiten zur Frage des Verbalaspekts im Englischen'. In Schopf (1974a), pp. 248–307.

Seiler, H. (1952). *L'aspect et le temps dans le verbe néo-grec.* Paris: Les Belles Lettres.

Serebrennikov, B. A. (1960). *Kategorii vremeni i vida v finno-ugorskix jazykax permskoj i volžskoj grupp.* Moscow: Izd-vo AN SSSR.

Seuren, P. A. M. (1974). Introduction to P. A. M. Seuren, ed., *Semantic syntax.* Oxford: Oxford University Press. Pp. 1–27.

Šewc, H. (1968). *Gramatika hornjoserbskeje rěče,* **1**, *fonematika a morfologija.* Budyšin (Bautzen): Domowina.

Sommerstein, A. H. (1973). *The sound pattern of Ancient Greek.* Oxford: Basil Blackwell, for the Philological Society.

Stevenson, C. H. (1970). *The Spanish language today.* London: Hutchinson University Library.

Thomas, E. W. (1969). *The syntax of spoken Brazilian Portuguese.* Nashville, Tennessee: Vanderbilt University Press.

Trubetzkoy, N. S. (1939). *Grundzüge der Phonologie.* Travaux du Cercle Linguistique de Prague **7**.

Tschenkéli, K. (1958). *Einführung in die georgische Sprache,* **1**, *Theoretischer Teil.* Zürich: Amirani Verlag.

Vendler, Z. (1967). 'Verbs and times'. In Z. Vendler, *Linguistics in philosophy.* Ithaca, New York: Cornell University Press. Pp. 97–121. (Revised version of Z. Vendler, 'Verbs and times', *The Philosophical Review* **66** (1957), 143–60.)

Verkuyl, H. J. (1972). *On the compositional nature of the aspects.* Dordrecht: Reidel.

Vogt, H. (1971). *Grammaire de la langue géorgienne.* Oslo: Universitetsforlaget.

References

Walter, H. (1973). 'Die Tempus-, Modus- und Aspektsemantik der finiten Verbformen in der modernen bulgarischen Literatursprache', *Zeitschrift für Slawistik* **18**, 198–212.

Welmers, Wm. E. (1973). *African language structures*. Berkeley: University of California Press.

Wright, W. (1898). *A grammar of the Arabic language*, **2**. Third ed., revised by W. R. Smith and M. J. de Goeje. Cambridge: Cambridge University Press.

INDEX

absolute state, *see* state, absolute
accomplishment, 44n.
achievement, 43
Akan, *see* Fante
Akkadian, 78n.
aktionsart, 6n.
Albanian, 110n.
Ancient Greek, *see* Greek, Ancient
aorist(ic), *see* past, perfective, *and individual languages*
Arabic, 2, 9, 13, 18n., 78–81, 82
  morphology, 95, 98, 115
aspect, definition of, 1–6, 15
atelic, 14, 44–8

Baltic, 88, 89, 91, 93, 94; *see also Latvian, Lithuanian*
Balto-Slavonic, 83, 88–92, 94; *see also Baltic, Slavonic*
Bantu, 128; *see also* ChiBemba, Shona, Swahili
basic meaning, 11, 38
Bemba, *see* ChiBemba
Bulgarian, 7n., 66–70, 74f., 125f., 131n.
  Aorist and Imperfect, 13, 21, 23, 26, 31f., 71
  markedness, 118, 119f.
  Perfect, 62, 107–10 *passim*

Celtic, 39, 99f., 106; *see also individual languages*
Cheremis, 110n.
ChiBemba, 128
Chinese (Mandarin), 22, 59, 88, 94, 101, 102, 128
  -le, 2, 19f., 58, 81f.
completion, 18–21, 44–8, 59n., 63, 64, 132
constative, 113f., 118f., 120
context, influence of, 3, 20, 45f., 79f., 82f., 113, 118–22

contingent state, *see* state, contingent
continuous, 12, 13, 25f., 33, 34, 38, 51
cumulative-distributive, 24n.
Czech, 27n., 66, 67, 70, 107, 108

delimitative, 22n.
distributive, 24n.
durative, 14, 22, 41–4 *passim*, 48
Dutch, 99
dynamic situation, 13, 14, 35, 48–51; *see also* nonstative

English, 1, 3, 4, 124f., 132f.
  Habitual, 25, 27–30 *passim*, 72, 103
  nonfinite forms, 2, 39f., 55
  Perfect, 5f., 52–61 *passim*, 107
  Perfect and time reference, 54–6, 60f.
  Present tense without present time reference, 68, 69, 73, 77
  Progressive, 15, 34–40 *passim*
  Progressive, forms, 9, 87, 99, 103
  Progressive, markedness, 112, 113f., 122
  Progressive Perfect, 62f.
  Progressive and stative, 36–9, 49n.
  prospective, 64f., 106
  punctual, 42f.
  telic, 44–8 *passim*
  verbal particles, 89, 93, 94
Estonian, 108f., 110
event, 13, 20, 47f., 51
existential perfect, *see* perfect, experiential
experiential perfect, *see* perfect, experiential

Fante, 57, 106
feature analysis, 129, 130–2
Finnish, 8, 108, 110n.
formal expression, 6–11, 14, 87–110; *see also* morphology, syntax

Index

French, 60, 68f., 73f., 78, 106, 126f.
Imperfect, and Past Definite, 1, 3, 4, 13, 17, 21, 22, 26, 27, 34, 42, 45n., 46
Imperfect and Past Definite, forms, 95, 96, 98
Perfect (Compound Past), 53, 61, 107, 108
periphrastic Progressive, 9n., 33, 87, 99, 103, 122
frequency, 111, 116f., 118
future, 2n., 18, 22n., 64f., 66–71, 73, 92
future perfect, 8n., 53, 56, 108

Gaelic, see Irish, Scots Gaelic
general factual, see constative
general meaning, 10f., 38
Georgian, 100f., 124
Aorist and Imperfect, 12, 21, 32, 114, 115, 116, 120
Perfect, 62, 108, 109, 110
Perfective and Imperfective, 26, 32, 67, 70f., 74
Perfective and Imperfective, forms, 88, 92f., 94, 98
German, 8, 53, 60, 86n., 107, 131n.
verbal prefixes, 46f., 89, 91n., 93, 94
Germanic, 83, 90, 99, 107; see also individual languages
gesamtbedeutung, see general meaning
Gothic, 90n., 94
grammaticalisation, 6–10
Greek, Ancient, 14, 67, 95–7, 127, 131
Aorist and Imperfect, 12n., 17–22 passim, 50, 95–7, 98, 114, 121f.
Perfect, 53, 57, 62
Greek, Modern, 26, 61f., 63, 95–7, 98, 127
grundebedeutung, see basic meaning

habitual, 25f., 26–32, 50n., 72f., 82n., 103
and other aspectual values, 33f., 69f., 76, 120
Hindi, 85f., 102, 107f.
historic present, see present, narrative
Hittite, 83
Hungarian, 43, 66, 93, 94, 123

Icelandic, 32, 35, 37n., 99
Igbo, 82f., 101, 106, 120, 122
imperfect, see habitual, imperfective, past, and individual languages
imperfective, 1, 3, 4, 16f., 24–6
and locative, 98–103, 129f.
and stative, 51, 82–4, 122
and telic, 46–8
and tense, 78–82, 121

implicature, 28–30
inchoative, see ingressive
indefinite perfect, see perfect, experiential
Indo-European, 71–3 passim, 83f., 84–6, 97, 114, 120; see also individual subfamilies and languages
Indo-Iranian, 83, 85, see also individual languages
inferential, 108–10
ingressive, 19, 20, 132
internal structure of situation, see temporal constituency, internal
Irish, 84, 103f., 106
Progressive, 32, 39, 99f., 102
Italian, 1, 3, 53, 61, 107, 115n.
Progressive, 32, 33, 36, 73, 102, 112, 114, 115, 117
iterative, 27f., 30, 31f., 42–4 passim, 132

Komi, see Zyryan
Kpelle, 57, 59, 101f.

Latin, 46f., 74n., 89, 127
Perfect and Imperfect, 13, 53, 71, 83, 107n.
Latvian (Lettish), 91, 110n.
lexicalisation, 6, 7n.
Lithuanian, 25f., 27n., 91, 94, 119
localist theory, 129f.
locative expressions, 98–106, 129f.
Lusatian, Upper, see Sorbian, Upper

Macedonian, 88, 107
Mańśi, see Vogul
Mari, see Cheremis
markedness, 21, 62n., 63, 111–22
meaning, see semantics
inherent, 7n., 22, 23f., 41–51
model-theoretic semantics, see semantics, model-theoretic
Modern Greek, see Greek, Modern
morphology, 7n., 9, 46f., 53
individual languages, 19n., 23, 62, 87–98
and markedness, 114f., 116, 118f., 121f.
mutual, 24n.

narrative present, see present, narrative
nebenbedeutung, see subsidiary meaning
Nenets, 110n.
neutralisation, 55, 116
nonfinite constructions, 2, 39f., 55
nonstative, 7, 12, 34–9, 41, 51, 72
and tenseless languages, 82f., 122; see also dynamic situation
nouns, 40n., 45, 47

Old Church Slavonic, 12, 89, 90, 115n., 126

past, 55f., 58, 82–4, 85; *see also* perfect
  and habitual, 25f., 28–30, 72f.
  and perfective, 9, 12, 13, 22f., 71–3
  recent, 54n., 60f., *see also* perfect of recent past
perdurative, 22n.
perfect, 5f., 12, 52–64, 81, 84–6, 106–10
  experiential, 54, 58f., 62
  of persistent situation, 60, 62
  of recent past, 60f., 62, 106
  of result, 56–8, 59, 110
perfective, 1–5 *passim*, 12, 13, 16–24, 130
  and internal temporal constituency, 21, 46
  and iterative, 27, 31, 32
  and perfect, 12, 62–4 *passim*
  and stativity, 19f., 50f., 72, 82–4, 122
  and tense, 13, 66–71, 78–82
Persian, 86, 88, 114, 121
phase, 48f.
phonology, 111n., 116n., 117, 118n.
pluperfect, 8n., 53, 56, 58, 108
Polish, 66, 70, 108
Portuguese, 23, 34, 35, 62, 102, 104f.
present, 39f., 60, 66–71, 72, 82f.; *see also* perfect
  narrative (historic), 73–8
process, 13, 36f., 47f., 51, 72
progressive, 12, 15, 20, 32–40, 49n., 50, 73, 77
  forms, 9, 87, 98–103, 129f.
  and markedness, 112, 114
  and other aspects, 11, 22f., 25f., 30, 62
prospective, 64f., 106
punctual, 17f., 26, 41–4, 97f., 50, 51
Punjabi, 102, 107f.

recent past, *see* past, recent
relative time reference, *see* time reference, relative
resultative, 20; *see also* perfect of result, telic
Romance, 126
  Imperfect and Simple Past, 1, 74, 114, 115, 121
  Perfect, 11, 53, 61, 107; *see also* individual languages
Romanian, 53, 61
Russian, 125, 130–2, 133
  aspect and locative, 105, 130
  forms, 88, 89f., 97f., 107
  Habitual, 27, 28, 29f., 31, 72
  Imperfective, 1, 3, 4, 26

internal temporal constituency, 17, 18, 22, 23f., 41f., 50
iterative, 27, 31
markedness, 112n., 113, 115–22 *passim*
nonpast, 66–71 *passim*, 75f.
perfect meaning, 54, 58, 63, 84f., 107, 108
Perfective, 1, 3, 4, 17–24 *passim*
Perfective and completeness, 19, 20f., 46, 48
prospective, 65
punctual, 43

Sanskrit, 85
Scots Gaelic, 39, 99f., 102, 103f., 106
semantics, 6–11, 89–93 *passim*, 112–14, 116, 122, 131–2; *see also* basic meaning, general meaning, subsidiary meaning
  model-theoretic, 129, 132f.
semelfactive, 27n., 42, 43
Semitic, 78n., *see also* Akkadian, Arabic
Serbo-Croatian, 66–70 *passim*, 75n., 88
Shona, 102
simple denotative, *see* constative
situation, 13; *see also* individual kinds of situation
Slavonic, 1, 14, 16, 94, 128
  Habitual, 27, 72
  inherent meaning, 7n., 42, 43
  markedness, 21, 112–14 *passim*, 114–15 *passim*, 118–20
  Perfect, 107, 108
  verbal prefixes, 88–91; *see also* individual languages
Slavonic, East, 66; *see also* Russian
Slavonic, South, 67, 94; *see also* individual languages
Slavonic, West, 66; *see also* individual languages
Sorbian, Upper, 31n., 88
Spanish, 104f., 115, 122, 127
  Imperfect and Simple Past, 1, 3, 7, 9, 12, 19, 25, 71, 117
  Perfect, 6, 53, 54, 61, 107
  Progressive, 9n., 22f., 32–5 *passim*, 73, 102, 112, 114
state, 13, 20f., 34–9, 48–51, 57f., 72
  absolute, 104f.
  contingent, 38f., 49n., 103–5
stative, 50f., 82f., 86, 103, 132
  and individual aspects, 11, 19, 20, 34–9, 57f., 62, 122
subsidiary meaning, 11, 38
Swahili, 57
syntax, 9, 52, 87f., 98–110, 111n., 112n.

Index

telic, 44–8
temporal constituency, internal, 3,
  12, 16f., 21–4, 44, 52, 81
temporal restriction, 16f., 22, 37, 38f.;
  see also state, contingent
tense, 1–6, 9, 53, 66–84, 91, 94–8, 115,
  120, 131; *see also individual tenses*
tenseless languages, 72, 82–4, 120f., 122
terminology, 5n., 10, 11–13, 97f.
time reference, 1–6, 9, 18, 67–9, 78–84, 120
  adverbial, 54f., 56n., 60f., 79f.
  relative, 2, 39f., 52f., 55f., 58, 79–82
Turkic, 110n.; *see also* Turkish
Turkish, 108, 128

Udmurt, *see* Votyak

Upper Sorbian (Lusatian, Wendish),
  see Sorbian, Upper
Urdu, 102, 107f.

Vogul, 110n.
voice, 84–6, 97
Votyak, 110n.

Welsh, 104n., 106, 108
  yn+verbal noun, 11, 25, 39, 99f.
Wendish, Upper, *see* Sorbian, Upper

Yoruba, 82f., 87, 101, 120, 122
Yurak Samoyed, *see* Nenets

Zyryan, 110n.